NEW MONEY FOR HEALTHY COMMUNITIES

NEW MONEY FOR HEALTHY COMMUNITIES

Thomas H. Greco, Jr.

1994

Thomas H. Greco, Jr., Publisher
P.O. Box 42663 Tucson, Arizona 85733

ISBN 0-9625208-2-9

Thomas H. Greco, Jr., Publisher
P.O. Box 42663
Tucson, AZ 85733

Cover design by Randy Harris

Printed and bound in United States of America

ACKNOWLEDGMENTS

It is with great humility that I present this work, knowing full well that I "stand upon the shoulders of giants." I must acknowledge my debt to scholars and independent thinkers from the past who dared to question the orthodox views. Their dedication and persistence have encouraged my own work, and their keen insight and clear thought have enabled me to find my way through the maze of modern economic confusion and monetary obfuscation. Foremost among these giants is E.C. Riegel, whose penetrating analyses and lucid descriptions have provided the primary foundation for my current understanding of money and exchange. Others who must be mentioned are Ralph Borsodi, Silvio Gesell, Hugo Bilgram, Walter Zander, and Frederick Soddy.

Among my contemporaries, I wish to acknowledge the pioneering exchange experiments of Michael Linton, Bob Swann, and Paul Glover. Their efforts have advanced the cause of equity and freedom. I am grateful to each of them for their friendship, and for the exchange of views which we have enjoyed over the years.

With regard to the preparation of this manuscript, there are many whom I wish to thank:

Karen Kennedy for her continuous encouragement and assistance with early and late drafts of the manuscript; Mary Lin and Laura Till for editorial assistance and critical comments; Greg Meadows, Fred Foldvary, Al Andersen, and Stephanie Mills for critical comment and suggestions about the content of the book; Michael Linton and Bob Swann for reviewing particular chapters; Gordon Davidson and Phil Holliday for their reading of the complete manuscript; Neil Shafer for assistance in obtaining information about, and reproductions of, Depression-era scrip; Randy Harris for designing the cover; Mark Fockler for help with the illustrations; and Judy Knox and Matts Myhrman for proofreading the final manuscript.

Dedicated to all who dare to express their truth.

TABLE OF CONTENTS

LIST OF ILLUSTRATIONS AND EXHIBITS

PREFACE

This book is part of a continuing work which began in 1982. It was in that year that I first came to realize the fundamental importance of money and exchange mechanisms in determining how the world works (and doesn't work) and how these mechanisms define the very nature of human relations on every level.

My earlier book, *Money and Debt: A Solution to the Global Crisis*, explained the nature of money, identified the fundamental flaws in the current monetary and financial system, and suggested an approach to resolving the problem of exploding debt. It also laid out the foundation principles for the creation of both a more rational means of value measurement and more humane and equitable structures for mediating the exchange of goods and services.

New Money for Healthy Communities complements that earlier work. While *Money and Debt* deals more with general principles and global prescriptions, this present work is more specific and detailed, and has as its focus the local community and empowering action at the grass-roots level. *New Money for Healthy Communities* is a how-to-do-it manual. It describes exchange mechanisms which have worked in the past, as well as some of the more successful contemporary local exchange efforts. It identifies the pitfalls to be avoided, and it proposes specific methods for transforming the exchange process, methods which are rational, equitable, and empowering, and which can be easily implemented at the local level by small voluntary groups.

It is the author's hope that this information will be widely disseminated, and his belief that its wide application will assist humanity's struggle toward a more harmonious and happy world.

PART I MONETARY REALITIES AND OFFICIAL ILLUSIONS

CHAPTER 1 TOWARD A NEW WORLD ORDER

"Money will decide the fate of mankind."
-- Jacques Rueff[1]

Gaia Consciousness and Human Unity

The past 25 years or so seem to have brought a new period of enlightenment in which humans in increasing numbers have become aware of their oneness as a species, and their place, not as dominator or controller of nature, but as an integral part of the whole web of life. Many cultures have held the view that Earth is a living being in which each living species plays a vital role. It is a view which is now becoming current in our own culture and which sees humans as the "global brain," the Earth's center of self-awareness.[2] This changing identity is beginning to have profound effects upon the way we live our lives and, if we allow it, can change the whole course of history. Imagine a world in which war and abuse are only dimly remembered, in which there is no starvation, in which harmony among the species prevails and the rape of the earth has ceased.

In order for such a condition to come about, we must believe that it is possible; then we will find the way to make it happen, for "faith is the substance of things hoped for."[3] Our actions emerge out of our visions

---

[1] Title of the Introduction in Jacques Rueff's, *The Age of Inflation*. Tr. A. H. Meeus and F. G. Clarke, Chicago: Henry Regnery Co., 1964.

[2] This is best exemplified in the Gaia Hypothesis popularized by scientist James Lovelock and others. See, for example, *The Ages of Gaia*, *Gaia: A New Look at Life on Earth*, and *Healing Gaia*.

[3] Hebrews 11:1.

and ideals. We humans, in our role as co-creators with the "Higher Power," have plenty of work to do. There is work to be done at the personal level, confronting our own fears and doubts and taking responsibility for resolving our dilemmas; at the community level, using inevitable conflicts as opportunities to transcend our petty selves and limited perceptions; and at the societal level, building new structures which support and nurture rather than coerce and brutalize.

Economics drives politics, and money is the central mechanism through which economic power is exerted in the modern world. The history of the United States shows how power has progressively migrated from the people, local communities, counties, and states toward the Federal government in general, and the executive branch in particular. It is only through a study of monetary history, however, that a clear picture can be gained of how this has happened.

It is my firm belief that among the primary obstacles to the improvement of the human condition are the general reliance upon the current structure of global finance and the nature of its primary element, money. The dominating nature of these institutions is akin to that of the monarchies and ecclesiastical hierarchies of past eras. Their time is quickly passing.

New, transformational structures based on different values and assumptions are being developed. These structures need to be more equitable, democratic, and "ethereal."[4] They must be established in ways that promote the expression of values such as service, fairness, fellowship, and cooperation, rather than greed, privilege, and self-seeking. Thus, they will not compete with existing institutions, but develop in parallel with them, providing operational alternatives which can better serve the needs of people and the Earth, as the old order continues to decline.

---

[4] In the sense of "less substantial or material". Exchange media, representing individual choices and decisions, take the form, not of gold or silver, or even paper, but of ledger entries and electronic pulses moving with the speed of light from place to place. Such "electronic fund transfers" routinely take place in today's banking system, but the people's own credit is sold back to them for interest as if it were gold or silver.

Correcting Past Errors

Many of our fundamental social contracts and conventions are based on notions which are erroneous and self-defeating. Among the most insidious of these are:

1. The belief that the universe was created for humans and that mankind should dominate creation and manipulate it for his own ends; that nature is an enemy to be subdued and controlled.

2. The division of people into classes or castes -- "us" and "them"; "nobles" and "peasants"; "aristocrats" and "commoners"; elites who are suited to govern and the masses who must be governed; clients who are defective and need to be "fixed" and professional fixers who are certified as competent to do the fixing.

3. The belief that it is just for a majority, in the name of government, to coerce the conscription of either person or property for the use of the state.

4. The belief that land and natural resources, which are the common heritage of all humans (and indeed, all life on Earth), can be treated in the same way as other property, to be bought and sold, to be used or abused, and to be held as an object for speculative gain.

5. Belief in the efficacy of the practice of granting to a few the privilege to create money based on debt and to charge interest for its use.

It is the last of these which is our main concern here. As I see it, the foundation of state power and centralized control in today's world is the power to create and manipulate the medium of exchange. Because money has the power to command resources, and because most of us take it for granted, those few who control the creation of money are able to appropriate for their own purposes vast amounts of resources without being seen. The entire machinery of money and finance has now been appropriated to serve the interests of centralized power.

The key element in any strategy to transform society must therefore be the liberation of money and the exchange process. If money is liberated, commerce will be liberated; if commerce is liberated, the people will be empowered to the full extent of their abilities to serve one another; the liberation of capital and land and the popular control of politics will follow as a matter of course. Once equitable exchange mechanisms have been established it will no longer be possible for the privileged few to appropriate the major portion of the land, productive resources, and political power. This volume, therefore, focuses specifically on the creation and control of money, money substitutes, and alternative exchange mechanisms.

Subsequent chapters will describe the nature of money, its uses and misuses, the processes by which individuals and communities have been disempowered, and some local responses which have been effective in restoring community control in the face of centralized power. They will outline gentle strategies by which communities can establish sustainable, ecologically sound, local economies using "home-grown" exchange media and participatory methods for the allocation of capital.

CHAPTER 2 WHAT IS MONEY?

"Money is an information system we use to deploy human effort."
-- Michael Linton

The Essential Nature of Money

Definitions

The question, "What is money?" may seem trivial to us, who in this modern day make constant use of it, but it is confusion about the essence of money which has allowed it to be abused and misallocated. Money in classical economics is defined as (1) a medium of exchange, (2) a standard of value, (3) a unit of account, (4) a store of value, and (5) a standard of deferred payment. There are many problems with these definitions, but their primary inadequacy is that they are *functional* definitions; they tell what money **does**, not what it **is**. We need to understand the basic *essence* of money. Once we have grasped its essence we can begin to design exchange systems which will equitably serve the needs of people and the Earth.

The process of economic exchange always involves two parties. The fundamental exchange process is the barter exchange. When Smith delivers to Jones a sack of flour and Jones gives to Smith a bushel of apples in return, a complete barter transaction has occurred. Both parties are satisfied, and both have profited from the exchange. The problem with simple barter, of course, is that Jones may want Smith's flour, but he may have nothing that Smith wants. In that case no trade can be made. The fundamental purpose of money is to transcend this limitation of barter. Bilgram and Levy assert that:

> "We should ... define money as *any medium of exchange adapted or designed to meet the inadequacy of the method of exchanging things by simple barter.* Anything that accomplishes this object is 'Money.'"[5]

---

[5] Bilgram, Hugo, and L. E. Levy, *The Cause of Business Depressions*. Philadelphia: J. B. Lippincott Company, 1914, p. 95.

So money is a "medium of exchange" which transcends the limitations of barter exchange. But what constitutes a medium of exchange, and how can one trading partner get what he wants, even though he has nothing wanted by the other? Bilgram and Levy go on to explain:

> "The one quality which is peculiar to money alone is its general acceptability in the market and in the discharge of debts. How does money acquire this specific quality? It is manifestly due solely to *a consensus of the members of the community to accept certain valuable things, such as coin and certain forms of credit, as mediums of exchange.*"[6]

We can see then that the essence of money is an **agreement** (consensus) to accept something which in itself may have no fundamental utility to us, but which we are assured can be exchanged in the market for something that does.

Michael Linton, the originator of an exchange system called "LETS" (Local Employment and Trading System), has provided us with an essential definition of money. Linton defines money as "an information system we use to deploy human effort."[7] This is a profound revelation and if we think about it, it becomes clear that our acceptance of money is based upon its informational content.

Whatever we use as money, then, carries information. The possession of money, in whatever form, gives the holder a claim against the community of traders. The legitimacy of that claim needs to be assured in some way. The possession of money should be evidence that the holder has delivered value to someone in the community, and therefore has a right to receive like value in return, or that the holder has received it, by gift or other transfer, from someone else who has delivered value.

---

[6] *ibid.*

[7] The LETSystem will be described in detail in Chapter 10.

Historical Forms of Money

Historically, many different forms of money have been used. But the forms of money in common use have, over time, become progressively less substantial and more ethereal. In earlier times, certain useful commodities were used as money. These included such things as salt, cattle, grain, and tobacco. Tobacco was a common form of money in colonial America. Commodity money carries value within itself making it easy for traders to evaluate its soundness. The use of commodities as a medium of exchange really amounts to *indirect barter*. Such commodities can serve the exchange function because they are useful in themselves and generally in demand. I may have no use for tobacco myself, but if I know that it can be easily traded, I may accept it in payment when I sell my goods or services.

The use of precious metals as money is no different in nature from the use of any other commodities. Gold and silver came to be widely used as money because they provided the advantages of greater convenience and durability, especially when stamped into coins of certified weight and fineness.

Later, it became more common to use paper notes and base metal coins which were symbolic representations of commodity money, typically gold or silver, and could be delivered to the issuer who would exchange them for the metal they represented. Modern banking developed on the basis of issuing paper currency against "fractional reserves," *i.e.*, the banks issued more paper "claim checks" than they had gold to redeem.

Commodity money and redeemable paper have progressively given way to non-redeemable notes, bank credit, and computerized accounts, which while offering certain advantages, are easier for issuers to abuse and more difficult for traders to evaluate.

Today, most of the money is in the form of bank credit, with a small percentage also in the form of circulating paper notes of the central bank, which in the United States is the Federal Reserve Bank. These notes, however, are merely a physical representation of money which first emerged as bank credit and later was exchanged for paper.

The Money Circuit

Money flows in circular fashion. In order to apprehend the meaning of money one must first recognize this essential fact, that money has a beginning and an ending; it is created and it is extinguished. This is depicted in Figure 2.1, which shows money in the ideal. Money is first created by a buyer who issues it to a seller as evidence of value received. The money issued may be thought of as an I.O.U. which the buyer uses to pay for the goods and services he bought. That I.O.U. might be passed along from hand-to-hand as each recipient in turn uses it to pay for his/her own purchase. Eventually, it must come back to the originator of the I.O.U. who redeems it by selling something of value.

As an example, consider the process depicted in Figure 2.1. The originator, Mr. Able, buys something of value from Mr. Baker. He gives Mr. Baker his I.O.U. as evidence of value received. Baker then uses the I.O.U. to buy something from Mr. Cook, who, in turn uses it to buy something from Ms. Drew. The I.O.U. may continue to change hands any number of times as others use it to buy and sell (as indicated by the dashed lines between Ms. Drew and Mr. Young), but eventually, it must return to Mr. Able. At that point, Able has fulfilled his commitment to redeem the money he issued (the I.O.U.). He does this by selling goods or services equal in value to those which he received when he made his original purchase, accepting as payment his own I.O.U., *i.e.* the money which he originally created.

Now think of a group of traders who agree to accept each other's I.O.U.'s as payment in trade. Suppose they design a standardized form for their I.O.U.'s so that they are indistinguishable from one another. These standardized I.O.U.'s can take whatever form the community of traders has agreed to use for this purpose. They may be in the form of paper certificates, metal tokens or coins, or simply numbers in an account ledger. Each member of the group obtains a supply of these standardized I.O.U.'s or notes of fixed denomination, which s/he can now spend into circulation.

Now the originator, Mr. Able, instead of using his own personal I.O.U. to pay for his purchase, gives Mr. Baker standardized notes (I.O.U.'s).

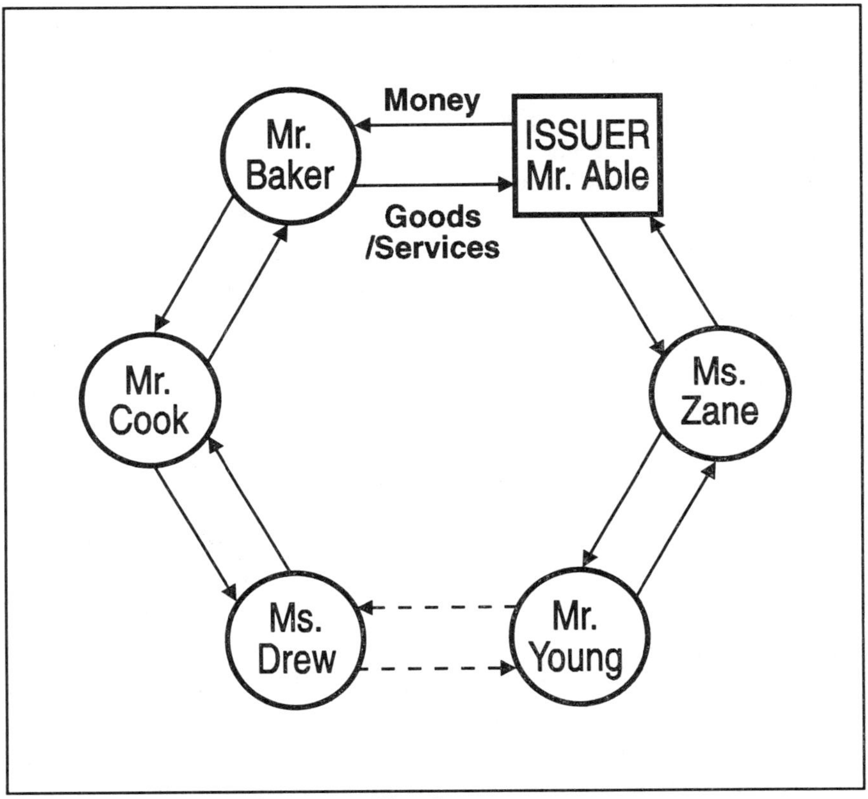

Figure 2.1: The Ideal Money Circuit

As before, Mr. Baker, then uses that money to buy something from Mr. Cook, who, in turn, uses it to buy something from Ms. Drew, and so on. Mr. Able is still committed to redeem the notes he issued and must eventually sell something, accepting as payment notes equivalent in amount to those he originally issued by buying.

This conceptualization of money is further elucidated by E. C. Riegel's excellent exposition:

> "Money simply does not exist until it has been accepted in exchange. Hence two factors are necessary for money creation: a buyer, who issues it, and a seller, who accepts it. Since the seller expects, in

> turn, to reissue the money to some seller, it will be seen that money springs from mutual interest and cooperative action among traders, and not from authority. That the Government can issue money for the people ..., is an utter fallacy. Money can be issued only by a buyer for himself, and he must in turn be a competitive seller to recapture it and thus complete the cycle.
>
> "A would-be money issuer must, in exchange for the goods or services he buys from the market, place goods or services on the market. In this simple rule of equity lies the essence of money."[8]

Riegel conceived a "private enterprise money" which closely conforms to this ideal.[9]

In the current system of banking, however, an originator of money must first obtain authorization from a commercial bank before he can put money into circulation. Typically, this is done by making an application for a "loan." The bank will evaluate Mr. Able's "credit-worthiness" and the value of his collateral. Let's say that Able offers his farm as collateral against the "loan." He signs an agreement known as a mortgage, and, in turn, the bank then credits his account for so many dollars representing the principal amount of the loan. This is depicted in Figure 2.2. In effect, Mr. Able gives the bank a legal claim (the mortgage) to his farm in return for standardized I.O.U.'s (bank credit or cash notes) which others will accept as payment for purchases. In terms of the prevailing practice, he has obtained authorization to write checks or draw cash up to the amount of his "loan."

Mr. Able, as before, has obligated himself to the community to redeem, by selling, the same amount of money he issued by spending. But, in

---

[8] E. C. Riegel, *Flight From Inflation: The Monetary Alternative*, The Heather Foundation, Box 4, Waterford, VA 22190, 1978. pp. 15-16. Any serious student of money and exchange should read this entire volume, but especially Chapter 2, which explains the essential nature of money.

[9] E.C. Riegel, *Private Enterprise Money: A Non-Political Money System*. New York: Harbinger House, 1944.

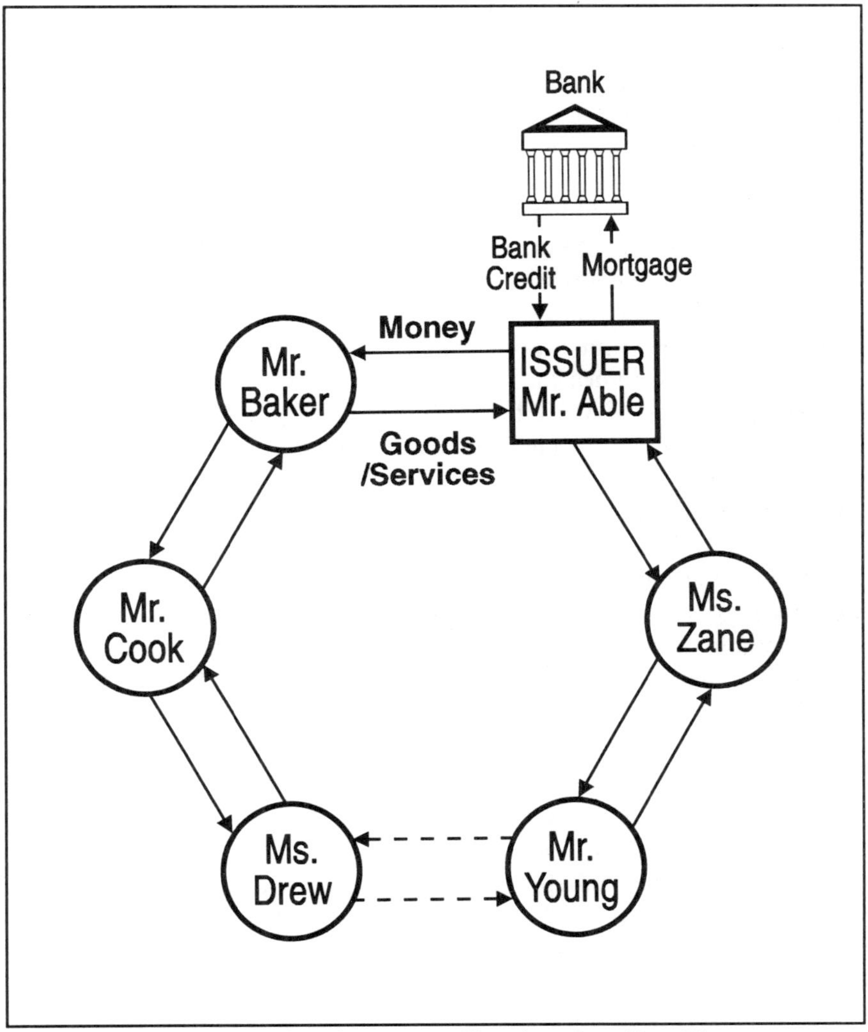

Figure 2.2: The Bank Credit Money Circuit -- Lending Phase

addition, he has also obligated himself to return to the bank the amount of money he "borrowed," *plus interest*. Thus, he must make sales sufficient to recover not only the amount of money he issued ("borrowed"), but he must also obtain an additional amount in order to pay the interest. If he is successful in doing so, he can reclaim his mortgage from the bank; if not, he loses his farm. When he repays the bank, the money he issued is extinguished. The redemption phase of the process is depicted in Figure 2.3. Note that the diagram shows a dashed line labelled "interest" coming to Mr. Able from outside the circuit and going to the bank.

In this scenario, Mr. Able is still the issuer, not the bank. The bank has not really loaned anything; it has simply converted the value of Mr. Able's farm into negotiable form. It has used its legal authority to "create" money by adding so much credit to Mr. Able's checking account or giving him the equivalent amount in the form of Federal Reserve Notes in return for his mortgage or I.O.U. The extra amount of money required of Mr. Able to pay the interest is not available within the circuit; it can only come from some other similar circuit, *i.e.* money issued by some other trader ("borrower") who has also gone in debt to the bank. If that happens, the second borrower will not be able to earn back enough money to redeem his mortgage. Thus, the charging of interest on the bank "loans" upon which new money is based causes a deficiency of money in circulation, preventing some debtors from earning back enough to redeem their collateral. Thus, the prevailing system guarantees that there will be a steady parade of losers.[10]

It is one thing for those who have earned money to charge interest for its use; it is quite another for banks to charge interest on newly created money based on debt. In the latter case the money supply must be continually expanded in order to prevent economic stagnation. In the prevailing monetary milieu, the federal government has assumed the role of perpetual borrower. By monetizing part of the government budget deficits, the Federal Reserve (commonly called the FED) prevents the supply of money from lagging too far behind the growth of "debt" incurred by private "borrowers." The prevailing monetary policies of the FED will determine whether money is "easy" or "tight," *i.e.*, whether monetization of government debt will be sufficient to provide private "borrowers" with the amounts of money needed to pay their "debts," or whether it will fall short. These actions by the FED are

[10] This point will be discussed further in Chapter 4.

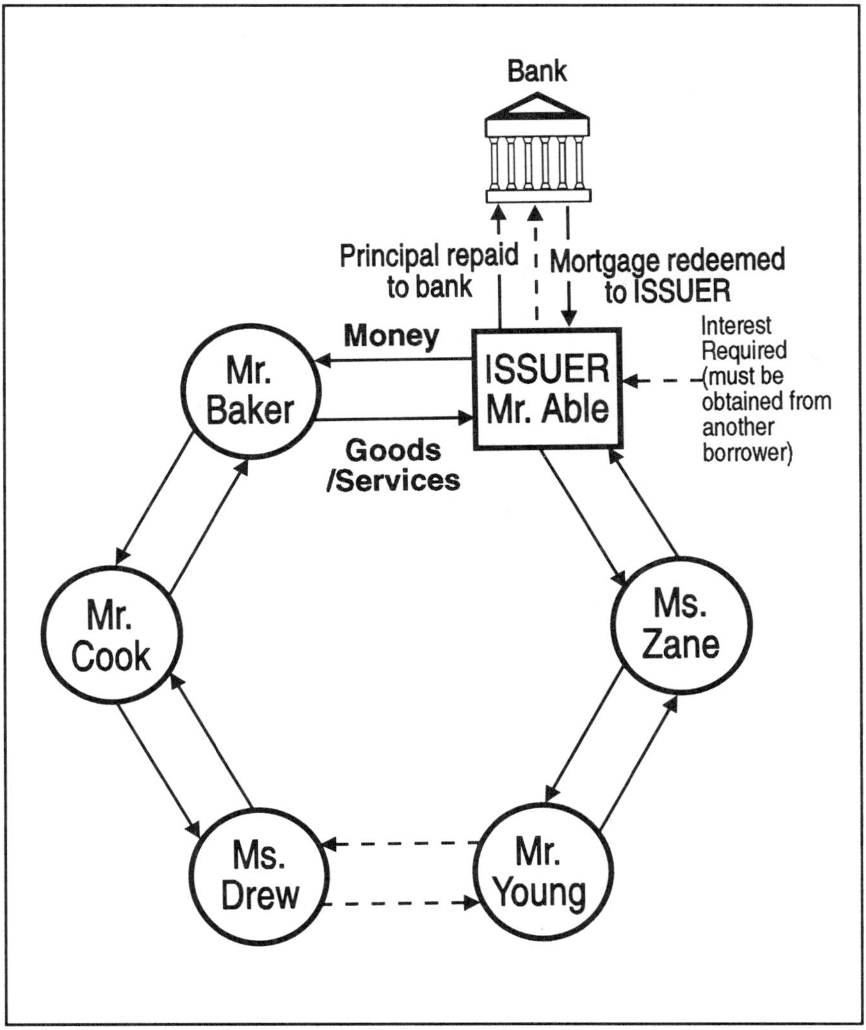

Figure 2.3: The Bank Credit Money Circuit -- Redemption Phase

largely responsible for the "business cycle" and periodic inflation and depression.

CHAPTER 3 THE POWER AND PLACE OF MONEY

"Money has become a ring we wear through the nose."
-- Mark Kinney

The Power Inherent in Money

The power of money lies in the fact that in any modern industrial society it is readily accepted in exchange for whatever one may want. This is potentially liberating as it promotes specialization of work, which in turn provides greater personal satisfaction and economic efficiency. When a person is able to do that work which s/he most enjoys and is most skillful at, both the individual and the community benefit. In the ideal, anything which facilitates exchange enhances the ability of everyone to meet their needs; in practice, it may not work out that way.

The use of money is a collective phenomenon to which each individual becomes habituated very early in life. Even children of 4 or 5 know that their material desires can be satisfied by taking money to the shops. It is a social convention deriving from our collective mentality -- our values, attitudes, and beliefs. A major aspect of our social conditioning in modern western culture is our preoccupation with the physical aspect of our existence and our alienation from nature and from our species identity (the human "oversoul"). The creation and use of money have been perverted as money has become an instrument of power. This has come about through the monopolization of its creation and the political manipulation of its distribution which makes it available to the favored few and scarce for everyone else.

To possess money is to possess power, for with money one may induce others to conform to his will. So money has become, as Mark Kinney describes it, "a ring we wear through the nose," which allows us to be led around by whoever controls it. There will always be a few "tethered bulls" who will find the strength and the will to break free, but our **collective** liberation will result from understanding how we are controlled by money and from acting to change the structures of money.

The Place of Money in Human Interaction

That is not to say that money or the use of money is inherently evil; on the contrary, the proper kind of money used in the right circumstances is a liberating tool which can allow the fuller expression of human creativity and the fuller realization of a dignified life for everyone. Those who like to quote the Bible on this subject usually quote it incorrectly. It does **not** say that money is the root of all evil. It says, "**the love of money** is the root of all evil."[11] But the word "money" in this context actually is more accurately rendered as "riches" or "wealth," not money as we understand it as a medium of exchange. So the meaning of this verse is to caution us against the extreme pursuit of material riches.

Money, as the medium of exchange, has not lived up to its potential as a liberator. This is largely because it has been politicized and centrally controlled, but also because the use of money and markets has been extended into realms which are better served by other exchange mechanisms. For example, within the family and clan, where the relationships are close and personal, and nurturing is a central concern, needs are easily assessed, responsibilities are readily assigned, and altruism is generally expressed. In these contexts, free gift exchange and sharing, rather than buying and selling, are clearly seen to work best.

The use of money within the household, family, or clan unit would be destructive to the human processes which are normal and necessary to their health. Money is better suited to facilitating the more impersonal exchanges which need to take place **between** social units, *i.e.* as a mechanism for mediating imports and exports.

The human body is an apt analogy through which economic processes can be understood. Just as each cell has its own internal processes which exclude the blood, and blood facilitates the flow of nutrients between cells, so do the essential socio-economic units have internal processes which exclude money but use it effectively for transfers between them.

A primary economic unit may consist of a single household or a cluster of households. It is an economic entity within which all of the processes of production, exchange, and consumption take place. There is, of course, always a certain amount of importation and exportation of goods

---

[11] 1 Timothy 6:10.

and services, the nature and amount of which vary according to the needs and resources of the household or cluster.

A healthy society depends upon the health of each of the units of which it is comprised. A primary aspect of that health is a high level of complexity of internal function, which implies, in this case, a high level of personal, household, and community self-reliance. In our social ordering (and money is, of course, a social device), there should be no impediment to the free operation of the primary social unit as an economic entity. This means that restrictions of economic flows within or between units should be minimized. The taxation of exchange constitutes a major impediment and is a drag on the economy. Taxes on wages and retail sales should therefore be avoided.

CHAPTER 4 WHAT'S THE MATTER WITH MONEY?

"The process by which banks create money is so simple that the mind is repelled."

-- John Kenneth Galbraith

Money is the vital medium within which we live our economic lives, and it is the central element around which many of our interpersonal relationships are organized. It is no exaggeration to say that the quality and essence of our medium of exchange, our money, are crucial to the quality of our lives -- our social interactions, our personal priorities, our relationship to the earth, and our very ability to satisfy basic human needs. As water is to the fish, so money is to people. We are largely unconscious of it. But when the water is polluted, the fish sicken and die; when money is "polluted," our economy sickens and people suffer as their material needs go unmet.

Although the existing systems of money, finance, and exchange are severely flawed, few people understand the structural nature of these flaws, much less how they might be remedied. Most of us take money for granted. Oh, it occupies plenty of our attention as we try to get enough of it to make ends meet, but we don't normally stop to think about what it really is, where it originates, or how it comes into being. We pay a huge price for our ignorance. Money has become an urgent problem.

Since money is an information system, let us describe the fault in terms of the information which it conveys and explain why that information is inaccurate, incomplete, or false. Indeed, the present official monetary system has become a **mis-information** system. As the tightly controlled news media in totalitarian states are to a free and independent press, so is our monopolized and political system of money and finance to a system of free money and free exchange. Just as the news industry can be perverted into a propaganda machine to serve the interests of a dictatorial government, so has the finance industry been perverted into a machine of privilege to serve the interests of centralized power.

Symptoms of Disease

The symptoms are easily evident and our news media are daily filled with reports of them -- inflation; unemployment; bankruptcies; farm, home and business foreclosures; ever-increasing indebtedness and impoverishment; homelessness; and a widening gap between the "haves" and the "have-nots." These in turn probably account, in large measure, for a secondary level of social and environmental decay -- violent crime, suicide, drug and alcohol abuse, theft, embezzlement, along with land, water and air pollution. These are not accidents; they derive from the inadequacies and errors inherent in structures which humans have themselves created.

Three Ways in Which Conventional Money Malfunctions

Conventional money malfunctions in three basic ways: (1) there is never enough of it to serve the purposes for which it is created, (2) it is misallocated at its source, going, not to those who are most in need or who will use it most effectively, but to political power centers and those who already control large pools of wealth (like large corporations), (3) it systematically pumps wealth from the poor to the rich. Each of these will be explained in turn, but to do so we first we need to explain how money is created in the current monetary system.

How Money Is Created

Wealth creation and money creation are two entirely different things. Wealth is created by the application of human skills to natural resources in the myriad ways which produce useful goods and services. Planting crops, assembling computers, building houses, and publishing a newspaper, are all examples of the production of wealth. Money, on the other hand, is a human contrivance; it is a symbol created by a deliberate process involving entities called "banks of issue." In the United States, it is mainly the *commercial* banks which create the bulk of the money supply in the form of bank deposits (or bank credit).

That's right, most of our money consists of deposits in checking accounts. Only about 30% of the money supply is in the form of coins or circulating paper currency, the familiar Federal Reserve Notes which we use every day. According to the Federal Reserve Bank of Chicago:

"..currency is a relatively small part of the money stock. About 69%, or $623 billion, of the $898 billion total money stock in December 1991, was in the form of transaction deposits, of which $290 billion were demand and $333 billion were other checkable deposits."[12]

Even Federal Reserve notes, however, while printed by the United States Treasury, are put into circulation by the banking system which buys them from the Treasury for the cost of printing. Money gets created as bank credit. Paper notes may then be exchanged for bank credit whenever depositors prefer to have paper. Whatever amount of paper money is withdrawn from banks is debited against someone's bank account balance. Thus, even that part of the money supply which appears as paper currency, begins as bank credit.

The amount of credit money which the banking system as a whole can create, is determined by the policies of the Federal Reserve, the private banking cartel which has been given power over money in the United States. The share which is allocated to each individual bank is determined by the amount of deposits which a bank is able to attract from customers and use as "reserves."[13]

Banks act both as creators of money and as depositories of money. When you deposit your paycheck in a commercial bank the bank is acting as a depository. This money is then available for you to write checks against. But, the money which you deposited had to begin somewhere. You got it from your employer; your employer got it from a customer; the customer got it from his/her employer or customer; and so on back to the beginning. The important thing to understand is the nature of that beginning. Banks create money by making loans. The money which you received in your paycheck was created at the point

---

[12] *Modern Money Mechanics*, Federal Reserve Bank of Chicago, 1992, p.3.

[13] For an excellent and authoritative, down-to-earth description of how the Federal Reserve System works, see *Figuring Out The FED*, by Margaret Thoren, 1985, 1993; available from Truth in Money, Inc., P.O. Box 30, Chagrin Falls, OH 44022.

when the bank, acting as a creator of money (or bank of issue), granted a loan to someone and credited her/his account for the amount of the loan.

Here's the way it works. Company XYZ goes to a commercial bank and receives a loan to expand its business. The bank simply credits the account of Company XYZ for the amount of the loan. Where did the bank get the money to lend to Company XYZ? It didn't get it anywhere; it created it. Unlike savings banks, savings and loan associations, and other "thrift" or depository institutions, which primarily can only lend out money that has been deposited with them, commercial banks actually create money out of nothing and put it into circulation by making loans.

As the Federal Reserve itself describes it:

> "Debt does more than simply transfer idle funds to where they can be put to use -- merely reshuffling existing funds in the form of credit. It also provides a means of creating entirely new funds...
>
> "...a depositor's balance also rises when the depository institution extends credit -- either by granting a loan or buying securities from the depositor. In exchange for the note or security, the lending or investing institution credits the depositor's account or gives a check that can be deposited at yet another depository institution. In this case, no one else loses a deposit. The total of currency and checkable deposits -- the money supply -- is increased. New money has been brought into existence by expansion of depository institution credit. Such newly created funds are in addition to funds that all financial institutions provide in their operations as intermediaries between savers and users of savings."[14]
>
> "(All bank deposits, originally) come into existence as banks extend credit to customers by exchanging bank deposits for the various assets

---

[14] *Two Faces of Debt*, Federal Reserve Bank of Chicago, 1992, pp. 17-19.

> that banks acquire -- promissory notes of businesses and consumers, mortgages on real estate, and government and other securities."[15]

This is just an obscure way of saying that the bank credits your account for the amount of the loan, and you, in return, give the bank your promissory note or a mortgage on your house. Those instruments, promissory notes, mortgages, and securities, are assets to the banks. They are claims which the banks have against the property of its customers, but to the customers, they represent debts owed to the banks.

Why There is Never Enough Money.

Debtors are always required to pay interest on these debts. Thus, the commercial banks lend something which they create out of nothing, and then require that the "borrower" pay interest for the privilege. Not only that, but banks usually require that the borrower pledge some "collateral," which they will confiscate if the borrower fails to repay the loan. The principal amount is created at the time the loan is made, but the money to pay the interest due in subsequent periods has not yet been created. Thus, debtors, in the aggregate, are in an impossible situation of always owing more money than there is in existence. They must vie with one another for the available money in order to avoid defaulting on their loans and losing their collateral.[16]

The Federal Reserve unabashedly admits that it purposely tries to maintain the scarcity of money. It clearly states in one of its official publications the mistaken notion that "**Money...derives its value from**

---

[15] *The Federal Reserve System: Purposes and Functions*, Board of Governors of the Federal Reserve System, Washington, DC 1961, p. 7.

[16] A more complete but simple and straight-forward explanation of the money creation process is contained in *The Truth In Money Book,* by Theodore Thoren and Richard Warner; available from Truth in Money, Inc., P.O. Box 30, Chagrin Falls, OH 44022.

its scarcity in relation to its usefulness."[17] This may indeed be true for politicized and improperly issued money, but it is decidedly not true of money which is properly issued and subject to the discipline of the free market. If the central government and the financial sector claim a disproportionate share of the country's wealth, then, of course, they must limit the amount of money made available to everyone else. The current system is based upon the "myth of scarcity," but the world needs systems and structures which affirm the truth of an abundant universe. That does not mean structures which allow inequity and waste, but structures which are efficient and which allow enough latitude for all to satisfy their own real needs.

How Money is Misallocated.

Money, as it emerges from the banks which create it, is not distributed fairly because the allocation decisions are not made democratically but rather by elite groups of bankers who are not held properly accountable. They act in their own interests pursuing goals which are typical of any corporate business -- profit and growth. As Ralph Borsodi explained it:

> "It is a sad but outrageous fact that banking is conducted today as a business by men who label themselves businessmen -- which presumably means an enterprise conducted for profit. In its essential nature, banking is a profession, and like every profession should be conducted to render a service by men who's motivation is service first, last and all the time. They must, of course, be properly compensated for their work, but this, in its essence, should be a professional fee, not a business profit."[18]

The greatest abuses, however, derive from the politicization of money, banking, and finance. Banking and government have become intertwined

---

[17] *Modern Money Mechanics*, Federal Reserve Bank of Chicago, 1992, p.3.

[18] *Green Revolution*, Vol. 34, No. 10, December 1977. See Appendix A for a more complete statement of Borsodi's views of banking as a profession and his proposals for the reform of banking practice.

and mutually dependent. In return for its privileged position, the banking cartel must assure that the central government is able to borrow and spend virtually any amount of money it wishes. Despite their public protestations, the banking system will always "float" the necessary budget deficits of the central government, by "monetizing" the debt. What this means is that the banking system will create enough new money to allow the market to absorb the new government bonds which must be issued to finance the deficit. Thus, it allows the government to spend as much as it wishes without raising taxes directly. The result is inflation, which has been called a "hidden tax."

Economists often argue that inflation is caused by too much money in circulation. This would seem to refute the contention that money is chronically in short supply. The answer to this is that inflation is not caused by the amount of money per se, but by the fact that some of the money in circulation is improperly issued and misallocated. Such is the case when the banking system "monetizes" the government debt, as described above. This phenomenon will be discussed more thoroughly in Chapter 9.

The people have been cut out of the most important decision process, that of determining how the aggregate wealth of the nation, the fruits of everyone's labor, will be spent. Massive expenditures for weapons, military interventions, and legalized "bribes" to client governments, along with S&L and corporate bail-outs which benefit the wealthy, well-connected few and increase the gap between rich and poor, are but a few of the abuses.

How Money Pumps Wealth From the Poor to the Rich.

In this regard, I speak not of the very poor, who have little or no wealth-producing capacity, but of the vast majority of people who work for a living but have little or no financial net worth. The "debt trap" is the bane of that class of people. Debt within the current system is destructive in two ways, first because of the interest (usury) that must be paid for the use of money (bank credit), and secondly, because of the collateral which must be forfeited when the debtor is unable to make repayment.[19] The chronic insufficiency of money assures that there will inevitably be some forfeitures. It is interesting to note that the word "mortgage" derives from roots which mean "death gamble."

Everybody pays the cost of interest, even those who do not borrow directly. Interest costs are included in the price of everything we buy, whether it is provided by the business sector or the government. The production of whatever we buy must be financed in some way, and interest is the cost of using financial capital. Margrit Kennedy gives some examples which show the percentage of the cost which goes to pay interest on capital. Though her examples are drawn from her native Germany, it is clear that the pattern would be similar for all industrial nations, since their monetary and financial structures are all basically the same.

Kennedy shows that the cost of interest on capital, as a percentage of the fees paid by users were 12% for garbage collection, 38% for water, 47% for sewers, and a whopping 77% of rentals paid for public housing.[20] She also shows a comparison of the interest paid and the interest gained for the population of then West German households divided into 10 different income groups of equal size. This comparison indicates, as expected, that the lower income groups, because they tend to be net debtors, pay much more interest on their debts than they gain in interest on their investments. Indeed, the 80% of households having lower incomes, on average, pay more interest on their debts than they gain in interest on their investments. The highest 10% gain about twice as much

---

[19] For an explanation of the difference between usury and interest, see my earlier book, *Money and Debt: A Solution to the Global Crisis*, second edition, Thomas H. Greco, Publisher, P.O. Box 42663, Tucson, AZ 85733. 1990.

[20] Kennedy, Margrit, *Interest and Inflation Free Money*, Permakultur Institut e.V., Ginsterweg 5, D-3074 Steyerberg, West Germany, 1988. Fig. 3 facing p. 14.

interest as they pay, and the richest of these gain progressively more.[21]

Lending money at interest, either directly or through financial intermediaries is one of the primary mechanisms by which the rich get richer and the poor get poorer.

Money carries information, but the present monetary system is dysfunctional because it carries flawed information. If information is the essential quality of money, then the next logical question is, what kind of information does it, and should it carry? The answer which immediately presents itself is that money should carry information about "merit." If money allows its possessor to claim wealth from the community, what is the basis for that claim? The possession of money should be evidence that the possessor has delivered value to the community, and is therefore entitled to receive back a like amount.

If money is improperly issued though, the information which it carries is polluted at the very source. By issuing money to unproductive or privileged clients of the money monopoly, and by demanding interest (usury), the banking system redistributes wealth from producers to privileged non-producers. The consistent pattern of official action over the past several decades has been to concentrate economic power by centralizing control over the medium of exchange, limiting access to it, and charging exorbitant prices for its use (in the form of interest/usury).

---

[21] *ibid.* Fig. 4 facing p.15.

The Usury Trap

In his story, *The Financial Expert,* R. K. Narayan's main character is a man named Maragaya, a small-time money lender who conducted his business under a banyan tree outside the banking office. Maragaya was fascinated with the idea of compound interest. It was an idea which had served him well, not only in directly multiplying the money that he lent, but also in allowing him to acquire properties upon which he had made loans, for inevitably some of his clients were unable to repay him. This is the picture of the usury trap which Narayan vividly and movingly portrays.

> They (the peasant borrowers) went by the evening bus, but leaving their mortgage deed (with Maragaya), and carrying in their pouches three hundred rupees, the first installment on which was already held at the source. The first installment was the real wealth -- whose possibilities of multiplication seemed to stretch to infinity. This was like the germinating point of a seed -- capable of producing hundreds of such germinating points. Lend this margin again to the next man, as a petty loan, withholding a further first installment; and take that again and lend it with a further installment held up and so on.... it was like the reflection in two opposite mirrors.
>
> You could really not see the end of it -- it was part of the mystic feeling that money engendered in Maragaya, its concrete form lay about him in his iron safe in the shape of bonds, and gold bars, and currency notes, and distant arable lands, of which he had become the owner because the original loans could not be repaid, and also in the shape of houses and blocks of various sizes and shapes, which his way of buying interest had secured for him in the course of his business -- through the machinery of 'distraint'.
>
> Many were those who had become crazed and unhappy when the courts made their orders, but Maragaya never bothered about them, never saw them again. "It's all in the business," he said, "It's up to them to pay the dues and take back their houses. They forget that they asked for my help." People borrowed from him only under

stress and when they could get no accommodation elsewhere. Maragaya was the one man who easily lent. He made the least fuss about the formalities, but he charged interest in so many subtle ways and compounded it so deftly that the moment a man signed his bonds, he was more or less finished. He could never hope to regain his possessions -- especially if he allowed a year or two to elapse.

There were debt relief laws and such things. But Maragaya nullified their provisions because the men for whom the laws were made were enthusiastic collaborators in his scheme, and everything he did looked correct on paper.

-- R. K. Narayan, *The Financial Expert*[22]

---

[22] Narayan, R.K., *The Financial Expert*. Chicago: University of Chicago Press, 1981.

CHAPTER 5 THE DISINTEGRATION OF LOCAL ECONOMIES

"The way that a national economy preys on its internal colonies is by the destruction of community."

-- Wendell Berry[23]

The Historical Progression of Control Over Economic Input Factors

Control of human affairs is achieved primarily through the control of economic factors -- *economics drives politics*, and economic and political realities shape the structure of society. The long view of history shows a progression of control strategies which ruling elites have employed, applying their power in turn to each of the primary factors of economic production -- labor, land, and capital. Conquest, plunder, and enslavement remain to this day the dominant mode in international affairs. Blatantly brutal and gross political subjugation has declined in popularity, at least among the nations of the "civilized" West. The favored methods have become increasingly subtle, shifting from political domination of nation over nation to economic and financial domination of peoples by supra-national institutions. The "debt-trap" is neater than direct force but no less tyrannical.

Slavery is the direct control of labor through physical coercion and threat of harm. It has been commonly practiced throughout history, even in so-called "civilized" countries, and was a prominent feature of our own "free" country until just over a hundred years ago. As "civilization" has progressed, overt slavery has become both less palatable and less practical. Typical of the transition from direct control of labor to control over land was the passage of the "enclosure acts" in England. The elimination of the commons, upon which the vast majority of people depended for their livelihood, and the deeding of the land to the lords, deprived people of their means of living free and forced them to pay rent, usually in the form of crop shares. With land access restricted, and forced to pay onerous rents, people were increasingly driven from the land and into urban centers.

---

[23] "Does Community Have a Value?", in *Home Economics: Fourteen Essays*. New York: Farrar, Straus and Giroux, 1987.

With the advent of industrialization, the bulk of production shifted from the cottage and village, to factories and cities. Then, the control of capital -- the tools or means of production -- increasingly became the method of social control. Separated from their land and their tools, individuals were forced to work for money as a means of livelihood. For most, this meant migrating to the cities and selling their labor to the factory owners. These factors caused the evolution of what is commonly known as "wage slavery."

While wage slavery yet remains, the mechanisms of privilege and control have become even more subtle still, so subtle that few people have even the slightest idea of what is happening. Besides the economic factors of labor, land and capital, there is also a supra-factor which mediates and controls the process of exchange and the interchangeability among the other three economic factors -- *that factor is money.*

As pointed out previously, money has over time become increasingly ethereal, *i.e.*, less substantial. For thousands of years, even up to the writing of the U.S. Constitution, the common substance of money was precious metals, mostly gold and silver. These commodities, typically in the form of coins, carried value within themselves. The only questions needing to be ascertained by traders in the marketplace were those relating to the weight and fineness of the metal tendered. The stamping of metal into coins provided a means of certifying these factors, thus further facilitating the process of exchange.

For reasons of convenience and safety, paper notes began to be used to represent ownership of metal. The exchange of paper notes in the marketplace then provided an easy way of exchanging the value inherent in the metal which was stored elsewhere. The paper had value because it could be exchanged for metal at the place where it was stored. As paper money became more common and acceptable, and as the need for exchange media began to exceed the amount of metal available, there was the temptation to issue more paper than there was metal to redeem it. This gave rise to what is known as "fractional reserve banking."

Fractional reserve banking is the practice of issuing paper notes in amounts which exceed the value of the stores of metal which they represent. Generally, these amounts were several times the value of the gold or silver held.

The abuses of paper money and fractional reserve banking soon created problems such as bank runs and bank failures. Governments, naturally enough, began to intervene to regulate and centralize banking, eventually themselves becoming the greatest abusers. They either began to issue paper money themselves or, as in the case of the United States, allowed the formation of a banking cartel (the Federal Reserve System), through which their profligate spending could be financed.

When the monetary abuses became apparent, people increasingly exercised their option to redeem their paper notes for metal, causing "bank runs" and "panics." Occasional runs on isolated banks, while disastrous for their depositors and investors, were not of great consequence to the general economy. The centralization of money and banking, however, did not end the abuses, but rather has institutionalized them to the point where the entire economy is adversely affected.

As their reserves of metal began to run low, governments and central banks had no other choices but to either stop their abusive issuance of paper money, or to rescind the redeemability feature. They have invariably chosen the latter.[24]

Through the development of a medium of exchange which can be created virtually out of nothing and allocated according to the values and objectives of those who have the money power, it is now possible for a small elite group, both in and out of government, to quietly and imperceptibly control the entire realm of human affairs. As Nobel prize

---

[24] It was at this point that the separation should have been made between the unit of account and the form of payment. The dollar, for example, as a unit of account, could have continued to be defined as the value of so much fine gold, while government and/or bank notes or credits might have been stipulated as the means of settling accounts. But the value of these notes and credits in terms of gold would have to be determined by the market, not by statute.

winner, Frederick Soddy has put it, "Money now is the NOTHING you get for SOMETHING before you can get ANYTHING."[25]

Social Control Through Control of Money and Finance

At the same time that money was becoming more etherealized, centralized, and politicized, market mechanisms were becoming a more dominant feature of economies at all levels. From the individual level, to the community level, to the regional level, and on up, economies have become increasingly specialized and therefore dependent upon market exchange. This predominant condition is in sharp contrast with many historical (and a few current) examples of local and regional economies characterized by versatility and self-reliance. Versatility derives from a diversity of skills and resources; self-reliance is based largely upon production for use as opposed to production for market, and the use of less formal internal exchange mechanisms.

Specialization of function is beneficial up to a point, and so is the market. The well-known economic concept of "comparative advantage," which provides the fundamental argument in favor of free trade, cannot be denied. Yet, the advantages of self-reliance and versatility at every level must also be acknowledged for both individuals and communities. If they are to avoid complete loss of control over their quality of life, they must also avoid becoming overly dependent upon existing markets in which the exchange media are monopolized and abused, and the mechanisms of finance are political and undemocratic.

---

[25] Frederick Soddy, *The Role of Money*, 1935. It is significant to note the context of this quotation, as well:
"The 'money power' which has been able to overshadow ostensibly responsible government, is not the power of the merely ultra-rich, but is nothing more nor less than a new technique designed to create and destroy money by adding and withdrawing figures in bank ledgers, *without the slightest concern for the interests of the community* (emphasis added) or the real role that money ought to perform therein..."
For more of Soddy's analysis of money and finance, see also, *Wealth, Virtual Wealth and Debt*. third edition, Hawthorne, CA: Omni Publications, 1961. Reprinted from the second edition, 1933.

For people living in industrialized countries, everything has become increasingly commodified. Even babies, human blood, and body parts have become objects of commerce. We have become increasingly dependent upon external and remote sources of supply for the most basic necessities of life. Most of us, when separated from our highly developed technology and intricate mechanisms of finance and transportation, lack even the most basic skills required to keep ourselves warm, dry, and well fed. Our alienation from the land, the basic tools of production, and each other, manifests in increasing environmental and social degradation.

Social Disintegration

Along with our increasing dependence upon remote and impersonal political and economic entities has come the disintegration of traditional social structures -- the family, the clan, the tribe, the village, and the bioregional community. All these have paled into economic insignificance, and, lacking economic power, they have become politically and socially impotent as well. Now, in this atomistic society, the wage earner's allegiance must be to his/her employer -- the corporation or the government bureaucracy. The majority of those who are not wage earners depend upon some form of government-granted privilege or transfer payment, such as mining rights, grazing and timber leases, farm price supports, and Social Security payments.

The social disintegration which we see seems somehow related to both the loss of freedom and the inability to participate effectively in the process of making the decisions which affect our lives. All the rhetoric about democracy and "government by the people" notwithstanding, freedom is today constrained in many subtle ways, both politically and economically.

A prime example of this in the political realm is the obvious "gerrymandering" of congressional and legislative districts. The drawing of the lines of these districts seems to be aimed, not so much at gaining advantage for one or the other of the two major parties, but at limiting the ability of various ethnic, economic and social classes to gain effective representation in government. This political homogenization limits the ability of legitimate interests to organize effective political power or even to have their issues and concerns debated in the political arena. The consequence is that only the corporate and monied interests are able to get their voices heard and influence the process of government.

Many countries in Europe and elsewhere have Parliamentary governments involving "proportional representation." They have numerous political parties representing particular interests. A party is able to gain representation in Parliament in proportion to the percentage of the votes it receives in an election. Thus, even a small minority party can gain representation with as little as 5% of the votes. Far from being divisive, this assures that various points of view will be heard.[26]

A basic factor which seems to underlie the limits both to freedom and effective participation is that of scale. As Chilean economist Manfred Max-Neef explains it:

> "It is absolutely impossible to have participation in a gigantic system; it can only occur at the human scale -- in other words where people have a face and a name, where they mean something to each other and are not simply statistical abstractions."

He goes on to say that the critical size of a participatory group will depend upon its function but, "in any case, .. will never be very large."[27]

---

[26] Perhaps the U. S. should consider basing congressional representation, only partly upon geography and more upon voluntary association. A person could choose the organization through which he/she would cast his/her vote. Each such association, which would have to be some minimum size, would be entitled to elect a representative.

[27] Manfred Max-Neef, "Reflections on a Paradigm Shift in Economics", in *The New Economic Agenda*. Mary Inglis and Sandra Kramer (Eds.), Findhorn Press, The Park, Forres IV36 OTZ, Scotland, 1985, p. 147, 148. Other works which deal more thoroughly with the theme of human scale are: *The Breakdown of Nations* by Leopold Kohr, E.P. Dutton, New York, 1957, 1978; and *Human Scale* by Kirkpatrick Sale, Coward, McCann & Geoghegan, New York, 1980.

If we are to reverse the trend of ever increasing alienation, we must begin to organize ourselves into small functional social groupings which empower their members and provide a meaningful level of mutual support.

CHAPTER 6 MONEY AND THE CONSTITUTION

"No State shall ... make any thing but gold and silver coin a tender in payment of debts; ... "

-- Article I, Section 10, U.S. Constitution

The original Articles of Confederation of the United States of America provided for a loose federation of thirteen sovereign states. This was seen by some to be inadequate for the destiny of the new nation as they envisioned it. The adoption of the Constitution was an attempt to strengthen the position of the federated states relative to foreign nations by delegating certain powers to the federal government, in particular, the power to declare war and the power to enter into treaties. The Constitution carefully spelled out the limits of federal authority, and sought to preserve the power of the states and of the people. Despite the care with which the powers of the federal government were enumerated, various interpretations by the courts over the years have allowed power to be increasingly concentrated at the federal level, and have given it permission to engage in activities which seem contrary to the intent of the Constitution.

Of special note are the agreements of the States with respect to money, which were written into the Constitution. Article I, Section 8, enumerates the various powers of the Congress. Among these is the power to "coin money, regulate the value thereof, and of foreign coin, and fix the standard of weights and measures."

In order to understand the meaning of this section, one must understand the prevailing situation and the parlance of that time. The form of money which we use now was not the form used back then. At the time of the writing of the Constitution, the substance of money was gold and silver coin, but now, almost all the money is in the form of bank credit, with the remainder in paper bills and base metal coins. Congress was given the power to stamp precious metals into coins of measured weight and fineness, and to decide how much metal was to be contained in the monetary unit, *i.e.* to "regulate the value of," the dollar. It was not given the power to print paper money or to create some other form of "legal tender."

The intent of the Founding Fathers is further clarified when we consider another part of the Constitution which listed certain limitations on the powers of the States. Article I, Section 10, provides that "No State shall enter into any treaty, alliance, or confederation; grant letters of marque and reprisal; *coin money; emit bills of credit; make any thing but gold and silver coin a tender in payment of debts; ...*"

The clear intention was to standardize coinage by placing that power in the hands of Congress. The required form of payment for debts was to be limited to gold and silver coins. Other forms of payment might be accepted by the payee but could not legally be required of the debtor, *i.e.* be made legal tender.

Bills of credit were promissory notes such as those which were issued by the Colonies (States), and which commonly circulated as money prior to the Constitution. The Colonies spent these notes into circulation, in quantities that were typically excessive in relation to the tax revenues available for their redemption. The eventual consequence of such abuse was that colonial currencies in the hands of the people lost much of their value, causing economic distress. During the Revolutionary period, the Continental Congress issued paper money, called "Continentals," which were similarly abused, thus derived the saying "Not worth a Continental."

By writing these provisions into the Constitution, the Founding Fathers sought to prevent a recurrence of these earlier monetary disasters. Although the federal government was not specifically prohibited from issuing bills of credit, this power was not specifically given to it either. In fact, an earlier draft of Article I, Section 8 included the power "to emit bills of credit" (paper notes), but it was deleted in the final version.

The Consolidation of Money Power

It is probably unconstitutional for Congress to do directly what is done through the Federal Reserve, *i.e.* issue money based on the government's promise to pay. The issuance of "Greenbacks" by the U.S. Treasury under Abraham Lincoln during the Civil War was just such a case in point. Lincoln, instead of borrowing from the banks at exorbitant rates of interest to finance the war, had the Treasury issue (spend) paper currency directly into circulation. These "greenbacks" were controversial throughout their entire life. While Lincoln managed to save the taxpayers the cost of interest by printing money instead of borrowing it, he usurped a power that the Founding Fathers had intended to withhold.

Subsequent to the end of the Civil War, the banking interests saw to it that such a costly (for them) move would not be repeated. They found a way for the Federal government to get what it wanted, namely the power to spend without limit, while enhancing their own wealth and power. Thus, the constitutional limitation upon the federal government with respect to monetization of its debt has been circumvented by its collusion with international banking interests to redefine and manipulate the exchange media (money) and its allocation within the economy.

This began with the National Bank Act of 1863 which required each bank to purchase a dollar amount of government bonds equal to one-third of its capital and surplus.[28] This collusion between bankers and politicians became more formalized with the establishment of the Federal Reserve System in 1913, and was legitimized by the subsequent entry of the United States into World War II. The Federal Reserve at that point announced a policy of providing the Treasury with the money needed to finance the war. It agreed to buy **any** amount of Treasury bills at the posted rate and to resell them at the same rate.[29] In the post-war era, the use of monetary mechanisms to handle fiscal (budgetary) indiscretions has come to be taken for granted. This, more than anything else, has undermined the democratic process in America, and allowed the emergence of the American Empire under elite control.

Over the years, the monetary authorities have managed to quietly redefine the dollar, from a specified weight of gold, to a unit of bank credit with no defined value. While the Federal government ostensibly controls the central bank (the Federal Reserve System) and regulates the banking industry, the reality is probably more the other way around.

---

[28] Dunkman, William, *Money, Credit and Banking*. New York: Random House, 1970, pp. 284,285.

[29] *ibid*, pp. 360-363.

Those who "pay the piper, call the tune." It is naive to think that political campaign contributions made by wealthy individuals and corporations do not buy influence. Not only has the power migrated from the local and state levels to the federal level, it has been privatized and appropriated by a monetary and financial ruling class.

Western civilization has reached a crisis point. The imperial stage of civilization is approaching its zenith. To permit its continued development to its ultimate maturity would be to permit a global tyranny far beyond Orwell's imagining, and to sell the soul of humanity into a new feudalism of material excess for some, comfort for a few, and subsistence and drudgery for most.

The single most important element needed to assure a future of freedom, dignity, health, and realization of the human potential, is the creation of non-political, equitable exchange media and the dispersal of financial power. The only feasible way to achieve this, I believe, is through the establishment, by private initiative, of community-based complementary exchange mechanisms which are democratically and locally controlled.

The End of Empires

Even though the dominant trend of civilization over the past several millennia has been toward increasing centralization of power in the hands of fewer and fewer people, there are signs that civilization may now be starting to move toward decentralization and local control. Even as the shadow of "Big Brother" looms ever larger and the prospect of global tyranny appears increasingly probable, we can see a major turn approaching.

Diverse networks of communication and mutual support are beginning to emerge. The village, neighborhood, household, farm and community are now becoming more significant as centers of education and economic activity. Manufacturing operations, while they are largely being shifted to lesser developed countries (LDC's), are at the same time, being decentralized. Many large companies are forming work teams which are given broad decision making power over their own work methods.

Information handling is increasingly becoming the substance of work, both inside and outside of the formal economy. Work styles are changing. More and more people are moving toward diversification of skills and self-employment. As cities grow larger and transportation channels become clogged, people are finding ways of working which are less stressful and more efficient. "Telecommuting" and home-based employment are becoming ever more common, especially among highly skilled workers and professionals.

Centralized institutions of power, even while appearing to further consolidate their power, are disintegrating from within. The world has been startled with the suddenness of the collapse of the Eastern Bloc and the Soviet Union, which once seemed monolithic and indestructible. Old ethnic identities are reemerging as the seeds around which a new order is beginning to crystallize. But even this degree of centralization around ethnic identities, with all their historic rivalries and animosities, will probably be transitory. With the emerging global consciousness and person-to-person communications, it seems likely that the nation state as the dominant political institution is in its last days.

It is important to recognize that economic, political and social structures are interdependent and mutually determining. They comprise the fabric of "culture." In our highly mobile and atomistic society we have grown dependent upon structures which are inimical to humane and liberative values. Any attempt to address the "mega-crisis," or to transform socio-economic realities, must come from a holistic perspective. The interconnections among land tenure, money, banking, finance and taxation must be thoroughly understood. Transformation requires not only a deeper understanding of the mechanisms of land speculation, money creation, and coercive wealth redistribution, but also a change in our basic assumptions and attitudes.

CHAPTER 7 RESTORING THE INTEGRITY OF PERSONAL AND COMMUNITY ECONOMIES

"Wage slavery will exist so long as there is a man or an institution that is the master of men; it will be ended when the workers learn to set freedom before comfort."

-- G. D. H. Cole[30]

Solutions to global problems require a global perspective and trans-global interaction, but it does not necessarily follow that we need to have a centralized global authority with coercive power to carry them out. Indeed, we have ample evidence to demonstrate that such centralized authorities lack sensitivity to local needs. The more remote the government, the less responsive it is. Competition among nation states has generally compounded human misery through war. What seems more appropriate to the current era is a pyramid of communication and cooperation with power vested in the small societal units which comprise its base.

Manfred Max-Neef in discussing a new paradigm for economics, enumerates nine fundamental human needs which fall into two categories -- *"having"* needs and *"being"* needs. They are the needs "for permanence or subsistence; for protection; for affection or love; for understanding; for participation; the need for leisure; for creation; for identity; and for freedom."

He points out that industrialized countries are better at providing for the "having" needs than they are at satisfying the "being" needs, while the lesser developed countries (LDC's) often do the opposite. He argues that it is possible to organize economic systems which can adequately satisfy the entire range of human needs.[31]

---

[30] Cole, G.D.H., and W. Mellor, *The Meaning of Industrial Freedom*. London: Geo. Allen and Unwin, Ltd., 1918, p.4. Quoted by Erich Fromm in *The Sane Society*, p. 249.

[31] Max-Neef, *op.cit.*, pp. 147-148.

Healthy Communities; Healthy World

The direction which needs to be taken to achieve this goal is toward structures and mechanisms which provide greater personal freedom and wider, more effective, participation. Since adequate participation is possible only within small groups, the emphasis must be upon the strengthening of local communities and voluntary associations. These will, in my opinion, form the foundation of a new world order which will be both sustainable and humane.

Healthy local economies, like healthy individuals, are characterized by a diversity of skills and resources and a large measure of self-reliance and self-determination. Economic empowerment will require some degree of de-coupling from the present global exchange system and the implementation of exchange media which are locally and democratically controlled.

The vogue in economic development strategies for many years has been to go out and find a major corporation to move into the area with some large facility that would bring new money into the community and create jobs. On the surface, this seems perfectly reasonable, but in many cases, there has been insufficient attention paid to the cost side of the equation. This is true especially when the costs come in social and ecological, rather than direct, financial terms. But even in financial terms, the experience of many communities has been less favorable than expected. With communities competing against one another, tax abatements and other concessions needed to lure companies often negate most, if not all of the benefits. Recognition of these costs, coupled with the costs of providing additional public services needed to support the new businesses, is causing many communities to take another look at the efficacy of the "recruitment strategy."

Two Fundamental Strategies

If not recruitment, then what? I believe that the emerging trend in economic development activity will be for communities to become more reliant upon their own resources, to place greater emphasis on quality of life, and to begin restructuring in areas which presently make them vulnerable to external factors such as the supply of money and bank credit, prevailing interest rates, and levels of State and Federal government spending in their area.

What practical steps can be taken to protect local economies from the distorting effects of external monetary and financial machinations, and restore some measure of local autonomy? There are two general ways to go:

1. Reduce reliance upon money and markets, and/or
2. Bring money and markets under local, democratic control.

An effective strategy will probably require some combination of the two. Reducing reliance upon money and markets implies a number of adjustments. On the personal level, it means becoming free of the consumerist mentality, distinguishing real needs from conditioned wants, eliminating expenditures which are induced by fear, becoming more diversified in one's skills and abilities, learning to do-it-yourself, make do or do without, and, above all, developing mutual support relationships with others of like mind. Communities must likewise take stock of their own resources and take steps to reduce the amount of value imported into the community, substituting local production for imports and thus reducing their need to earn cash by selling exports.

Small (and Local) Is Beautiful.

Even the poorest among us is able to exert some power through the purchase decisions which we make every day. Every dollar spent is a vote cast. It is important to recognize that, however much or little money one might have, the choices one makes in spending that money, carry a great deal of weight in determining not only the products and services which the market offers, but also the very quality of community life. Although price is one of the primary criteria to be considered, it is not the only one.

Some consideration should also be given to the question of where one should do business. The familiar aphorism that "charity begins at home" contains much wisdom. An appropriate corollary might be that "prosperity begins at home." The first might be interpreted as "deal with the problems closest at hand," and the second as "support the business efforts of your friends and neighbors."

Local businesses spend most of their revenues in the local area, while chain stores and absentee owners withdraw most of their revenues to other places, building up ever greater pools of capital which can distort economic relationships everywhere. While they may be able to offer lower prices, it is often a false economy. We must ask, at what price do they offer lower prices? It is often at the expense of the environment, poorer working conditions for employees, and depersonalization of human interactions.

Because they control so many jobs and so much revenue, large corporations and chain stores can make a community dependent upon them. They can dominate a community by their lopsided economic power which allows them to wield political power as well. They can buy political influence, negotiate tax breaks, and extort concessions on zoning, safety, and environmental regulations.

It is also becoming more apparent that continual growth and construction, while it may benefit some privileged elements in the community, such as land owners, builders, and real estate brokers, can often be detrimental to the community as a whole. There are several negative effects which need to be considered. First, there are the added costs for services and infrastructure -- fire, police, water, sewer, road construction and maintenance -- which may exceed any additional tax revenues. Second is the cost of living which may increase because of "gentrification" and the increased demand for housing and other limited local resources. Third is the quality of life costs -- increased traffic congestion and noise; air, land and water pollution; loss of farm, forest, meadow, and marsh land, and increasing anonymity and depersonalization.

Locally-owned businesses are more likely to use local suppliers, saving on transportation costs, reducing the environmental costs of transport, and stimulating local production. They are more likely to employ local people, and they contribute to the culture and uniqueness of a community.[32]

How to Bring Money Under Local Control

Later chapters offer several concrete proposals for bringing money and markets under local, democratic control. These proposals, which can be implemented at the local level by voluntary groups, attempt to incorporate the principles and ideals outlined previously. Some of these ideas have already been tried in some form and to some degree, while others, to my knowledge, are original.

The kinds of exchange systems implied by the above considerations are ones which are both self-regulating and independent of outside control by government or any other central power. To use an organic metaphor, they function autonomically. This implies a decentralized approach in which the creation and extinction of money (the symbol) is directly linked to the creation and transfer of value (the reality which money represents). In such systems the quantity of money (symbols) should adjust automatically to increases and decreases in the value and quantity of goods and services being traded. The process of money creation should be open and accessible, or, to use Ivan Illich's term, "convivial." It must also be debt-free and interest-free. If money were to become a symbol of merit from the very point of its creation, the producer of economic value would be properly rewarded for his/her effort and skill, and production would be encouraged. At the same time, production would be ecologically sound, since money, in a convivial system, is more readily available and has less power to induce people to act in self-destructive ways. Money would be the product of cooperation among individuals within integral communities.

---

[32] There is much more that might be said about this approach, but it is being adequately addressed by others. Good sources of information are:
1. Missouri Community Economic Development, 628 Clark Hall, University of Missouri, Columbia, MO 65211.
2. Oregon Marketplace, 1004 W. 23rd Ave., Suite 300, Portland, OR 97210.
3. Industrial Cooperative Association (ICA), Community Economic Development Program, 58 Day St., Suite 203, Somerville, MA 02144.

Community Banking and the Liberation of Money

One can perhaps envision two distinct types of exchange systems emerging concurrently. These will be complementary systems. One type will be limited, local, "soft" and "personal" system, along the lines of Michael Linton's LETS system (Local Employment and Trading System) which, in effect, monetize community credit. These will be referred to as "Mutual Credit" (MC) systems. Mutual Credit systems are intended to facilitate exchanges which are intermediate between the informal exchange processes of the family, clan or affinity group, on the one hand, and the formal, impersonal marketplace on the other. Mutual Credit systems are by nature "personal" systems, in that they operate among a relatively small group of people who have ready access to information about one another, and can therefore relate to one another on a personal basis.

The other type of system will be an extended, "hard" and "impersonal" system, necessary for exchanges between individuals in different social units and in trades between relative strangers. While these latter characteristics are also those of the present global monopolistic system, the transformed system which I envision will differ from it in significant ways.

At some point, however, it should be possible to "network" local currency and/or MC systems together into a web extending over a wide geographic area and including a very large total population. It could conceivably be a global network. This would then obviate the need for impersonal systems entirely.

It has been the stated goal of centrally controlled monetary systems to match the money supply to the needs of the economy, but the "needs" have never been well defined in monetary terms, and, as pointed out above, the mechanisms of control have never worked to benefit more than a relatively small privileged class. The supply of money or credit available at any given time should accurately reflect the wealth of material wares and services available for purchase in the near term. This is a principle which has been disregarded in modern money and banking, but must be heeded in establishing a healthy local exchange system.

Why Local Currencies?

The fundamental advantages of local currencies or credits are:

1. They can be spent only within the limited area of the community,
2. They can be created locally in accordance with the needs of the local economy, and,
3. They encourage local people to patronize one another rather than buying from outside the community.

When needs remain unfulfilled, the first question that needs to be asked is, is it for lack of skills, resources, or motivation, or is it because of lack of money? Much "good work" is left undone because those who have the will to do it lack the money, and much "bad work" is done because it is in the narrow self-interest of those with money to do it, and others, because they need the money to live, can be persuaded to do it too. The intentional scarcity of official money has a destructive effect which can be overcome by supplemental local currencies.

The supply of official currency is limited. It is created by entities external to the community which have little sensitivity to or concern for the needs of the local population. Official currency can and does circulate far and wide. It can easily be spent to buy goods and services from remote regions. Money spent outside the local community is no longer available to facilitate trading within the local community. It must be replaced by attracting money from outside, either by exporting products, receiving government transfer payments, or attracting tourists and businesses to come and spend.

The universality of national currency, its greatest advantage from the standpoint of flexibility and spendability, is also its greatest disadvantage from the standpoint of local self-reliance and economic integrity. Rather than the lack of skills or physical resources, local unemployment and business stagnation are more often the result of the fact that the money necessary to connect needs with supplies has gone elsewhere.

A local currency is, by its nature, limited in scope. It is recognized only within a limited area, and therefore can be created, earned, and spent only within that area. This fact tends to favor local producers who have agreed to accept it, and its narrow range of circulation makes it more likely that the spender will be able to earn it back. Local currencies, thus, stimulate local production and employment.

Just as a break-water protects a harbor from the extreme effects of the open sea, so does a local currency protect the local economy from the extreme effects of the global market, and the manipulations of centralized banking and finance. Complete reliance upon national currencies and the competitive conditions of the global market tend to force all communities to the lowest common denominator of environmental quality and working conditions. Local currencies, however, provide a buffer which allows local communities to set their own standards and maintain a high quality of life.

There need never be any scarcity of local currency since it is created by members of the community themselves in the course of trade. Any time two parties wish to make a trade they can do so even if they have no money. Local currency or credits can easily be created to enable the exchange to take place.

PART II LOCAL CURRENCIES PAST AND PRESENT

CHAPTER 8 A BRIEF HISTORY OF LOCAL CURRENCIES

> *"It seems axiomatic that whenever a government fails to provide an adequate supply of currency or coin to maintain commercial trade, the people will step in to provide their own to fill the vacuum."*
> -- Ralph A. Mitchell and Neil Shafer[33]

Scrip of The Great Depression

The Great Depression of the 1930's was a very important chapter in history. It provided a great many important lessons for civilization, many of which are yet to be fully grasped. Much has been written about the nature and causes of the Depression, which need not be repeated here, but for those for whom the event is too remote in time to have much meaning, we will attempt a brief summary.

The Great Depression was world-wide in scope, but it was particularly severe and long-lasting in the United States[34]. It was characterized by several concurrent financial and economic symptoms, which the U. S. Department of Commerce listed as follows:

1) an unemployed population estimated at over 12 million,
2) a serious agricultural situation resulting from excessive production, ruinous (low) prices, and large debts,
3) a financial and credit system in grave danger of collapse,
4) a large internal debt,
5) almost insurmountable barriers to foreign trade,

---

[33] Mitchell, Ralph A. and Neil Shafer, *Standard Catalog of Depression Scrip of the United States: the 1930s Including Canada and Mexico.* First edition, Iola, Wisconsin: Kraus Publications, 1984.

[34] *ibid.*

6) a perplexing foreign debt situation,
7) an unbalanced federal budget,
8) disorganized state and municipal finances,
9) increasing disorder and an almost complete lack of confidence on the part of the people.[35]

Most importantly, however, was the fact that there was little money in the hands of the people, and given their uncertainty about their prospects of getting more of it, people tended to hoard what little money they did have. Hoarding slowed the velocity of circulation, which further reduced the volume of business being transacted. Serious human needs went unmet -- until people began to organize.

Besides learning how to "make do, or do without," people began to establish mutual support structures, like workers' cooperatives, many of which would recycle and repair donated or broken items. People learned to share what they had, and to by-pass the market and financial systems. Most of these measures were considered stop-gaps to be utilized until things "got back to normal," but in some of them there seemed to be the promise of more permanent improvements. One of these "stop-gaps," which was intended to address the problem of the dearth of currency in circulation, was the issuance of "scrip."

History is full of examples of successful local initiatives aimed at providing exchange media, but the Great Depression of the 1930's saw this done on an unprecedented scale. There were literally hundreds of scrip issues that were put into circulation by a variety of agencies, including state governments, municipalities, school districts, clearing house associations, manufacturers, merchants, chambers of commerce, business associations, local relief committees, cooperatives, and even individuals. These issues went by different names, depending on who issued them and the circumstances of their issuance. Common scrip types were certificates of indebtedness, tax anticipation notes, payroll warrants, trade scrip, clearing house certificates, credit vouchers, moratorium certificates, and merchandise bonds.

---

[35] *ibid.* p. 13.

Caslow Recovery Certificates

Among these scrip issues there were many failures, but there were also many impressive successes. There is much to be learned from both the failures and the successes. One interesting case was the issuance, beginning in 1933, of "Recovery Certificates" by a Chicago newspaperman named Caslow. Figures 8.1 and 8.2 show the front and reverse sides, respectively, of a Caslow Recovery Certificate.

As can be seen from Figure 8.2, these notes were of a variety known as "stamp scrip," and were supposed to be "self-liquidating." The inscription on the face of the notes describes the basic terms of their circulation. A 2-cent stamp was supposed to be affixed on the back and signed by the buyer each time the note was passed on in a transaction. When all the stamp spaces had been filled, a one dollar note would have changed hands 54 times and facilitated $54 worth of business. The 54 stamps which had been sold and affixed would have provided $1.08 in official money, one dollar of which would presumably be used to redeem the note, and the remaining eight cents going to cover the expense of operating the plan.

While Caslow managed to gain wide acceptance of his scrip idea, it does not seem to have worked out quite as planned. Mitchell and Shafer relate the story as follows:

> "At first a small amount, it was manageable and fully accepted by a number of merchants. At one time over 500 stores were participating. Through his newspaper, "The Caslow Weekly," Caslow was able to form a large organization of self-styled "scrippers." The plan kept growing, and clubs, local clearing houses, etc., sprang up to take care of the scrip. The bulk of the scrip placed into circulation came through Caslow's using it to pay his workers. As for himself, he demanded cash for advertisements in his newspaper. As the scrip idea spread, as much as $30,000 might be issued in a single week. The plan failed, largely because there were too many field workers promoting the scrip plan and simply too much scrip. Around $1,000,000 was issued, and very little redeemed. After about two years, Caslow suspended publication of his newspaper and closed up

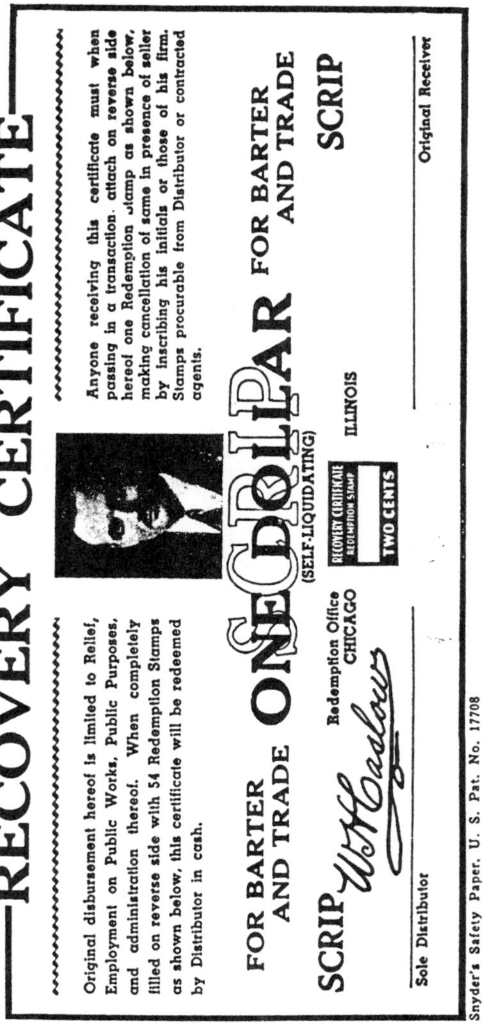

Figure 8.1: Caslow Scrip -- Face Side

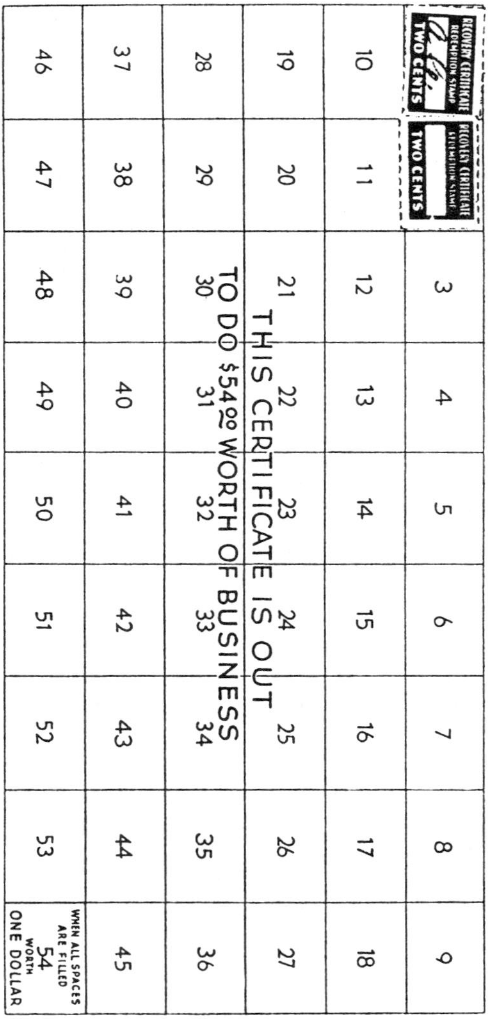

Figure 8.2: Caslow Scrip -- Reverse Side

shop."[36]

The obvious question which this story raises is, "What went wrong with Caslow scrip?" Why did a currency which enjoyed such widespread and strong support turn sour? Mitchell and Shafer do not provide enough of the details about its issuance or redemption to fully answer the question. They do, however, offer the opinion that there was "too much scrip." But was it simply a matter of too much scrip? I think this may be too simplistic an explanation. It begs the question, "too much in relation to what?"

Examination of the inscription on the face of the scrip makes several things apparent:

1. Caslow was the "sole distributor."

2. Stamps were "procurable from Distributor (Caslow) or contracted agents."

3. There is no mention of how the funds obtained from the sale of stamps were to be administered. It must, therefore, be presumed they simply went into the general fund of Caslow's business.

The eventual redemption of the scrip, therefore, seems to have depended entirely upon the integrity of Caslow and the solvency of his business.

We also note that the "Original disbursement hereof is limited to Relief, Employment on Public Works, Public Purposes, and administration thereof." This is rather vague and seems to be somewhat at variance with Mitchell and Shafer's report that "the bulk of the scrip placed into circulation came through Caslow's using it to pay his workers."

The self-liquidating feature works only if the note changes hands enough times to generate sufficient stamp revenue to allow the scrip to be redeemed for cash. Far more important are the conditions under which

---

[36] *ibid*, p.70

scrip is first placed in circulation and the commitment of the original issuer himself to accept it in trade.

I think the key to the failure of Caslow's scrip might be found in his refusal to accept it in payment for his own services (advertising). One of the fundamental rules of currency issuance is that the issuer be willing to redeem his/her own currency at face value (par), and that s/he be able to generate enough value in goods and/or services to redeem the issue at the rate of about 1% per day, which is equivalent to being able to redeem the entire issue in about 3 months time. More will be said about this question later on.

Larkin Merchandise Bonds

Another example, which was fairly typical of Depression scrip was one offered in 1933 by Larkin and Company of Buffalo, New York. Larkin was a large company with diverse operations including wholesale merchandising, a chain of retail stores and a chain of gasoline stations. When President Roosevelt declared his famous "bank holiday," the Larkin company issued $36,000 worth of "merchandise bonds" which it used to pay its employees.

Figure 8.3: Larkin Merchandise Bonds -- Face Side

Figure 8.4: Larkin Merchandise Bonds -- Reverse Side

As shown in Figures 8.3 and 8.4, these "bonds" consisted of certificates which bore the image of the company's founder and a guarantee that they would be accepted in payment for services or merchandise at any Larkin outlet in the U.S. The "bonds" were endorsed on reverse side and spent into circulation by the company. They were subsequently accepted by many Larkin customers and even other businesses. As the dearth of official currency eased, Larkin gradually retired the bonds. Company accountants estimated however, that while the bonds circulated, the original $36,000 issue had turned over enough times to allow the sale of $250,000 worth of merchandise, providing a significant boost to its business.[37]

Scrip was generally accepted and used to do business within a limited local area. The farther it got from home, however, the more uncertainty there was about its origin and the less confidence people would have in it. For this reason scrip tended to remain within the local economy and had the effect of stimulating local development and community

---

[37] This account was taken from *New Zealand GREEN$QUARTERLY*, issue 6, November 1991, which cites the original source as, *The Fig Tree*, "a Douglas Social Credit Quarterly Review", June 1937.

self-reliance. This limited range of acceptance might seem at first to be a disadvantage of scrip, but, from the standpoint of the local economy, it is a great advantage. Toward the end of the Depression, however, as official government and central bank currencies became more widely available, scrip disappeared.

Silvio Gesell and Stamp Scrip

Some of the most notable examples of successful scrip issues were instigated by Silvio Gesell, a successful German businessman who lived much of his life in South America, and who, at one point between the first and second World Wars, served briefly in the German government. Gesell, in his once famous book, *The Natural Economic Order*,[38] explained his views on the nature of money and how it functions in the economy, and outlined his ideas on how it should be reformed. He originated the plan for issuing a currency known as "stamp scrip." Later, the great American economist, Irving Fisher, became a proponent of scrip and wrote a book about it. His book, entitled *Stamp Scrip*, described some of the subsequent scrip experiments and outlined his recommendations for proper issuance of scrip.[39] His is one of the few handbooks available on the subject.

Depression-era Stamp Scrip in Germany and Austria

Among the most successful and famous applications of Gesell's stamp scrip idea were the ones which took place in the small Bavarian town of Schwanenkirchen and the Austrian town of Woergl.[40] Gesell's scrip was to consist of pieces of paper of uniform size (about 8 inches by 3.5

---

[38] Gesell, Silvio, *The Natural Economic Order*. San Antonio, TX: The Free Economy Publishing Co., 1934 (Translated from the sixth German edition). Originally published in 1913.

[39] Fisher, Irving, *Stamp Scrip*. New York: Adelphi Company, 1933.

[40] This historical information was derived primarily from two sources: (1) Richard Gregg, *The Big Idol*, Navajivan Press, Ahmedabad-14, India, 1963, and (2) Irving Fisher's *Stamp Scrip*, cited above.

inches) to be issued by a voluntary association of factories, merchants, a bank and any others. It would be issued in denominations of convenient amounts and be used in payment of wages and for trade. The shops who were members of the association would, of course, get all the trade. This would provide an incentive for other businesses to join, and business generally would improve.

Gesell's scrip was designed to have 52 spaces on the reverse side, one for each week of the year, and the scrip was to have the value of its stated denomination only for one week. In order for the scrip to maintain its face value, a stamp, costing two percent of the face value of the note, had to be affixed on the back, in the space allocated to that week. The stamps could be bought at the bank representing the association. This stamp device was supposed to keep the scrip from being hoarded, as people would try to spend it prior to the day the stamp had to be affixed and thus avoid the cost of the stamp.[41]

Gesell had many friends in Germany and his ideas were widely discussed but there was initially no attempt to implement them. At the time, shortly after the end of the first World War, there was currency inflation in Germany of astronomical proportions which caused severe hardships for the people. This inflation, like all inflations, was the result of improper and excessive issuance of official currency. It was part of a deliberate government policy to surreptitiously eliminate its debts by printing more money. This policy was probably a large factor in the eventual collapse of the German government, and helped set the stage for Hitler's rise to power, as he was one who exposed it.

With the coming of the Depression, the nature of the problem shifted. Money was then in short supply. Gesell's friend, Hans Timm, formed

---

[41] The idea of the stamp stemmed from Gesell's notion that the value of money should depreciate with time, just as does the value of the items which it is supposed to represent. This "gimmick" will indeed speed the velocity of circulation of the currency. However, if a currency or scrip is properly issued and its supply is not artificially restricted, there should be no incentive for hoarding. The "demurrage" which the stamp represents, then, would be unnecessary. This point will be further elaborated in subsequent sections.

an association for the purpose of implementing the scrip idea. Timm actually had printed such stamp scrip which he called *Wara*, a name derived by combining two words - "Ware," the German word for goods, and "Wahrung," the German word for currency. Timm's association was called the "Wara Exchange Association." *Wara* became fairly well known in Germany but it was never widely used.

The village of Schwanenkirchen had a population of about 500 and its only industry was a coal mine which had been closed for two years because of the depression. The village had barely existed by means of the government dole and almost everyone was in debt. Deflation throughout Germany led to bankruptcies, suicides and overcrowded jails. The coal mine owner had heard about *Wara* stamp scrip and decided to try it. He got a loan of official currency (Reichsmarks) and with it bought *Wara* stamp scrip from the Wara Exchange Association.[42] Then, according to a report in The New Republic for August 10, 1932:[43]

> "Herr Hebecker assembled his workers. He told them that he had succeeded in getting a loan of 40,000 Reichsmarks, that he wished to resume operations but that he wanted to pay wages not in Marks but in *Wara*. The miners agreed to the proposal when they learned that the village store would accept *Wara* in exchange for goods.
>
> When, after two years of complete stagnation, the workers for the first time brought home their pay envelopes, no one was interested in hoarding a cent of it; all the money went to the stores to pay off debts or for the purchase of necessities. The shopkeepers, too, were happy. Although at first they had felt a little hesitant about *Wara*, they had no choice, as no one had any other kind of money. The shopkeepers then forced it on the wholesalers, the wholesalers forced it on the manufacturers, who in turn tried to pass it on to those who carried

---

[42] This is another way of bringing scrip into circulation, but the use of official currency is not really necessary, as we shall explain later.

[43] Gregg, *op.cit.*

their notes, or they exchanged it at Herr Hebecker's mine for coal.

> No one who received *Wara* wished to hold it; the workers, storekeepers, wholesalers and manufacturers all strove to get rid of it as quickly as possible, for any person who held it was obliged to pay the 2 cent stamp tax. So *Wara* kept circulating, a large part of it returning to the coal mine, where it provided work, profits and better conditions for the entire community. Indeed, one could not have recognized Schwanenkirchen a few months after work had resumed at the mine. The village was on a prosperity basis, workers and merchants were free from debts and a new spirit of freedom and life pervaded the town."

Continuing the account in Fisher's words:[44]

> "The news of the town's prosperity in the midst of depression-ridden Germany spread quickly. From all over the country reporters came to see and write about the 'Miracle of Schwanenkirchen'. Even in the United States one read about it in the financial sections of most big papers. But no explanation was given as to the real cause of the miracle - that non-hoardable money was being tried out and that it was working marvelously."

Acceptance of *Wara* subsequently spread to various parts of Germany. About two thousand shops and one or two entire communities recovered by means of it. Finally, in November 1931, the German Government passed an emergency law ending the circulation of *Wara*. The "miracle" of Schwanenkirchen then ended and the town went back on the dole.

Another place where *Wara* succeeded was in the Austrian town of Woergl which, by 1932, was in dire straits. In this town of about four thousand people, many factories had closed and almost everyone in town had lost their jobs. A large amount of local taxes were unpaid. The mayor of the town had heard about *Wara* and decided to try it. In this

---

[44] Fisher, *op.cit.*

case, the *Wara* were issued by the town, in conjunction with a number of merchants and the local savings bank. The town paid its employees half in *Wara* and half in official currency.

Initially, some of the local merchants refused to accept *Wara*, but when they saw the trade going to the other shops, they too had to climb on the bandwagon. The *Wara* issue was a great success. Professor Fisher describes the situation this way:[45]

> "After the scrip was issued not only were current taxes paid (as well as other debts owing to the town), but many arrears of taxes were collected. During the first month alone 4,542 schillings were thus received in arrears. Accordingly, the city not only met its own obligations but, in the second half of 1932, executed new public works to the value of 100,000 schillings. Seven streets aggregating four miles were rebuilt and asphalted; twelve roads were improved; the sewer system was extended over two more streets; trees were planted and forests improved."

Unfortunately, this successful experiment was also ended under pressure exerted upon the Austrian government by the central bank. Figures 8.5 and 8.6, respectively, show the face and reverse sides of one of the Woergl notes.

To my knowledge, there is no current law which would prevent such initiatives as local scrip from being implemented today in the United States. The application of local exchange media could provide results every bit as dramatic as those obtained in Schwanenkirchen and Woergl.

Lessons Learned

Many of the scrip issues of the Depression era were defective in some way, and they should not be directly emulated, but the thing to be learned from this chapter in the history of money, is that it is possible for effective media of exchange to be issued at the local level and that

---

[45] *ibid.*

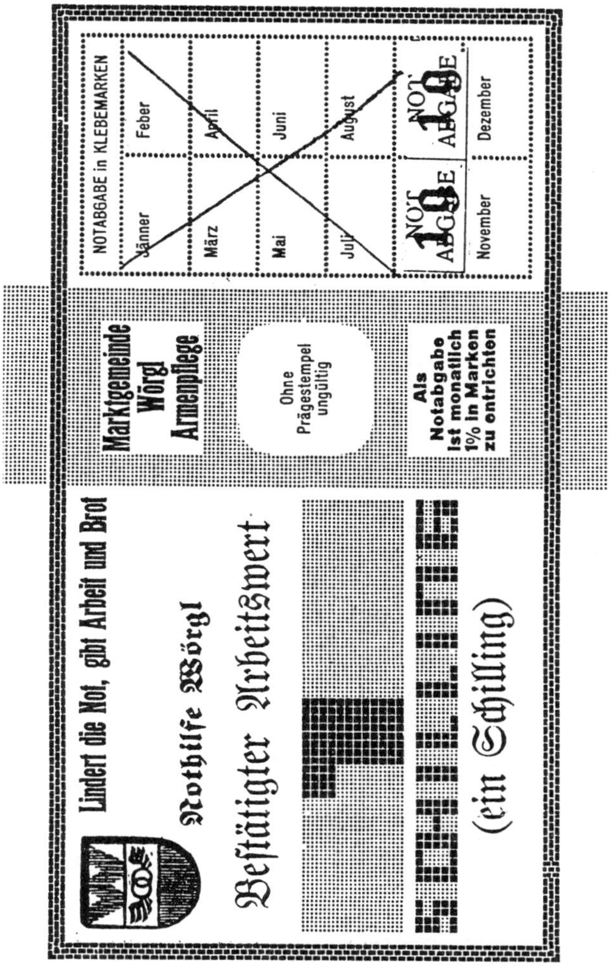

Figure 8.5: A Woergl Note -- Face Side

the centralized control of money and finance need not limit the ability of a local economy to preserve its own health.

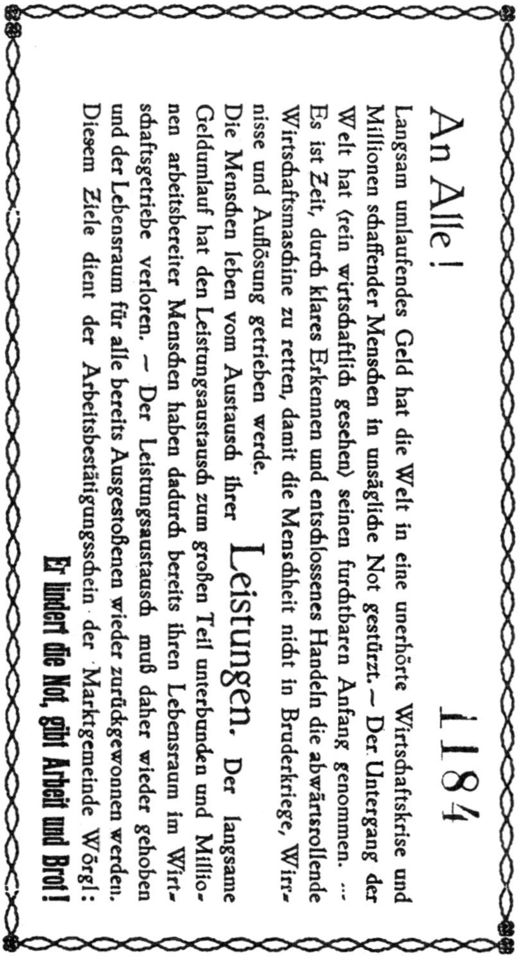
An Alle! 1184

Langsam umlaufendes Geld hat die Welt in eine unerhörte Wirtschaftskrise und Millionen schaffender Menschen in unsägliche Not gestürzt. – Der Untergang der Welt hat (rein wirtschaftlich gesehen) seinen furchtbaren Anfang genommen. – Es ist Zeit, durch klares Erkennen und entschlossenes Handeln die abwärtsrollende Wirtschaftsmaschine zu retten, damit die Menschheit nicht in Bruderkriege, Wirrnisse und Auflösung getrieben werde.

Die Menschen leben vom Austausch ihrer Leistungen. Der langsame Geldumlauf hat den Leistungsaustausch zum großen Teil unterbunden und Millionen arbeitsbereiter Menschen haben dadurch bereits ihren Lebensraum im Wirtschaftsgetriebe verloren. – Der Leistungsaustausch muß daher wieder gehoben und der Lebensraum für alle bereits Ausgestoßenen wieder zurückgewonnen werden.

Diesem Ziele dient der Arbeitsbestätigungsschein der Marktgemeinde Wörgl:

Er lindert die Not, gibt Arbeit und Brot!

Figure 8.6: A Woergl Note -- Reverse Side

Some scrip issues, of course, are more credible than others. The power, productive capacity and faithfulness of the issuer are factors which affect the credibility and market acceptance of a local scrip issue. The soundness and continued acceptability of a scrip issue are dependent upon its basis of issue, the amount issued, and the means by which issuance is regulated.

Scrip issued by municipal and state governments will have a high level of credibility if it can be used to pay taxes and fees, and is accepted at par with federal money. Such scrip is said to have a "tax foundation." Scrip issued by corporations, based on their own productive capacity, will have credibility to the extent that there is a demand for their products and their current assets are sufficient to "cover" the amount of scrip issued. Scrip issued by retailers in payment for their inventories of goods will have credibility because the goods are already there in the shops waiting to be bought. This is known as the "goods foundation" or "shop foundation" of scrip. Scrip issued by individuals is theoretically possible but its acceptability will depend upon the backing provided, usually in the form of real assets.

Economic depressions are typified by a scarcity of ordinary money. Indeed, most depressions are **caused** by restriction of the money supply by the monetary authorities. The subsequent felt lack of adequate payment media causes people to become fearful and to hoard what money there is. This hoarding slows its rate of circulation which further reduces the volume of business being conducted. Thus, the depression deepens until money becomes plentiful again. Replenishment of the supply of official (debt) money requires not only an increased willingness of the banks to lend, but also a willingness of individuals and businesses to borrow. Their recent experience of monetary stringency during a depression, however, makes them loathe to incur new indebtedness.

The prescription for addressing this dilemma, put forth by Lord Keynes, was for government to intervene by borrowing money and spending it into circulation. It was said that the temporary deficit thus incurred could be made up later by surplus revenues once the depression was over. The experience of 60 years has made it clear that the Keynesian prescription is flawed, that "later" never comes. As we have already explained, deficits become chronic because of the very nature of the debt-money system.

The original intent of using scrip was to provide a temporary supplement to scarce official currency. But the permanent use of a locally issued and controlled exchange medium, such as scrip, has clear advantages for insulating local economies from the distorting effects of global finance and banking.

Railway Notes

There have been numerous instances of public service companies issuing circulating notes and tokens. The familiar bus and subway tokens which are used in various places provide some idea of what might be possible. Most present-day instances of this kind intend only to provide a measure of convenience in regulating access and collecting the fares which are due.

There have been instances, however, in which tokens or notes issued by railway companies have circulated as money, being used as a means of payment, not only for railway services, but also for a wide variety of goods and services in the marketplace. According to Dr. Walter Zander, in his paper, *Railway Money and Unemployment*,[46] the Leipzig-Dresden Railway, sometime in the early 1800's, was authorized to issue one third of its capital in the form of "railway money certificates." These certificates, he says, remained in circulation for about forty years. Zander also indicates that during the 1920's, the German Railway issued a considerable amount of its own money.

Zander's own proposal, while apparently never implemented, was based on sound principles and makes eminent sense. My own proposals, which are outlined in later chapters, draw much of their inspiration from Zander's work and are consistent with it. While his proposal was aimed specifically at the German Railway, there is no reason why the same

---

[46] This paper, first published in 1933, proposed a new issue of railway money to help alleviate the effects of the Depression. This information was obtained from an English version published in Peace Plans #9 compiled by Libertarian Microfiche Publishing Company, Berrima, NSW, Australia. See the section, *Sources and Resources*, for the complete address.

rationale cannot be applied in proposing that any economic entity or consortium of producers be empowered to issue circulating currency.

The official monetary system puts the cart before the horse in that money must be obtained **before** a purchase can be made. Whether that money be in the form of paper, coins, or bank credit, its creation is beyond the control of the producers of real wealth. In other words, the creation of goods and services depends upon money changing hands. Zander's proposal is much more rational. It puts the horse properly before the cart, in that producers can create a form of money themselves with which to enable the purchase of their products. In this instance the creation of money depends upon goods or services changing hands.

When an economic entity, such as the Railway, must pay for what it needs in official currency, it must first acquire the currency to get what it needs. Alternatively it might purchase what it needs on credit in anticipation of having the cash it needs to pay at the time the bill comes due. However, in doing this, it commits itself to deliver something (money) which it only hopes to obtain. As Zander points out,

> "Whether its hope will materialize is uncertain. The undertaking to pay at maturity contains, therefore a speculative element, which is particularly hazardous in times of depression. But the railway can promise to pay something else, namely, to transport commodities and persons; that is to fulfill its function as a railway. There is nothing speculative about that. The means required for this, rolling stock and other plant, are available. This is therefore fundamentally different from a promise to pay cash at a future date, for in the latter case the means of payment have yet to be secured, and this by having transported passengers and goods. The capacity of the railway to act as a carrier is, on the contrary, unquestionable."

The essential features of the Zander plan are:

1. The Railway makes payment for goods and services, not in legal tender (central bank notes), but in transport certificates.
2. The Railway certifies that it will accept the certificates at their face value like ready money, in payment for its services.

3. The certificates are made out to the bearer.
4. They are issued in convenient denominations.
5. No one need accept them.
6. They have no legal value.
7. The market rate in relation to official currency is freely determined.

The primary feature in maintaining their value is the commitment of the Railway to accept the certificates at any time **at their face value**, regardless of their market rate.

Since the Railway certificates are not legal tender, traders in the market are free to refuse them or to accept them at a discount from their face value. The value of the certificates depends upon the ability of the Railway to deliver that which the certificates promise -- railway services. If the Railway should somehow over-issue, the market would react by discounting the certificates, *e.g.* accepting them at 95% of face value. This would tend to increase the demand for them among users of railway services, since they could now obtain a dollar's worth of service for only 95 cents. This would furthermore induce the Railway to reduce the amount of certificates in circulation. If it did not do so it would suffer a loss in profitability. It is in this way that a free currency is self-correcting.

The "Constant" Currency of Ralph Borsodi

In the early 1970's, Dr. Ralph Borsodi, political economist, social philosopher and founder of the School of Living,[47] together with a few

---

[47] Dr. Borsodi was the author of several books. One of his first, *This Ugly Civilization*, published in 1928, was widely read and anticipated the work of many of our contemporary social critics. Seeing the many social dysfunctions and unhealthy habits of the modern American lifestyle, Borsodi took his family to the country where they established a modern rural homestead. Much of this experience is documented in another of his books, *Flight From The City*. Borsodi founded The School of Living in 1934 to promote the further exploration of healthy living and healthy communities. Over the years, the School of Living has evolved into a nationwide educational

associates, developed and launched a currency experiment called the "Constant." Concerned about the chronic inflation resulting from official debasement of the dollar, Borsodi conceived a privately issued currency which would hold its value.

Borsodi's basic strategy for making his currency inflation-proof was to make it redeemable for a "market basket" assortment of basic commodities. The development of the Constant never progressed that far, but the Constants that were issued were backed by bank deposits of dollars. Constants circulated successfully for almost 2 years and enjoyed wide acceptance by the public. At its peak, the equivalent of about $160,000 in Constants was circulating throughout southern New Hampshire and elsewhere, both in the form of paper currency and as checking account balances at several area banks. News of the Constant was reported in several popular publications, such as *Forbes* and *Business Week*, in addition to numerous New England dailies.

Why Borsodi did not complete his plan for backing the Constant with commodities is not entirely clear. His advancing age and failing health may have been factors, along with possible organizational problems and lack of sufficient capital.[48] Figures 8.7 and 8.8 show the front and reverse sides, respectively, of a 25 Constant note.

---

network of people who are oriented toward personal responsibility, cooperative self-reliance, and ecological and social improvement. This author is a past President and Trustee of the School, as well as co-editor of its journal, *Green Revolution*.

[48] For a more detailed summary of the features of the Constant see Appendix C of *Money and Debt: A Solution to the Global Crisis*. For a complete description of the Constant experiment see Ralph Borsodi's, *Inflation and the Coming Keynesian Catastrophe: The Story of the Exeter Experiment With Constants*. Published jointly by The E. F. Schumacher Society, RD 3, Box 76, Great Barrington, MA 01230 and the School of Living, RD 1, Box 185A, Cochranville, PA 19330, 1989. The manuscript for this book was written in the early 1970's.

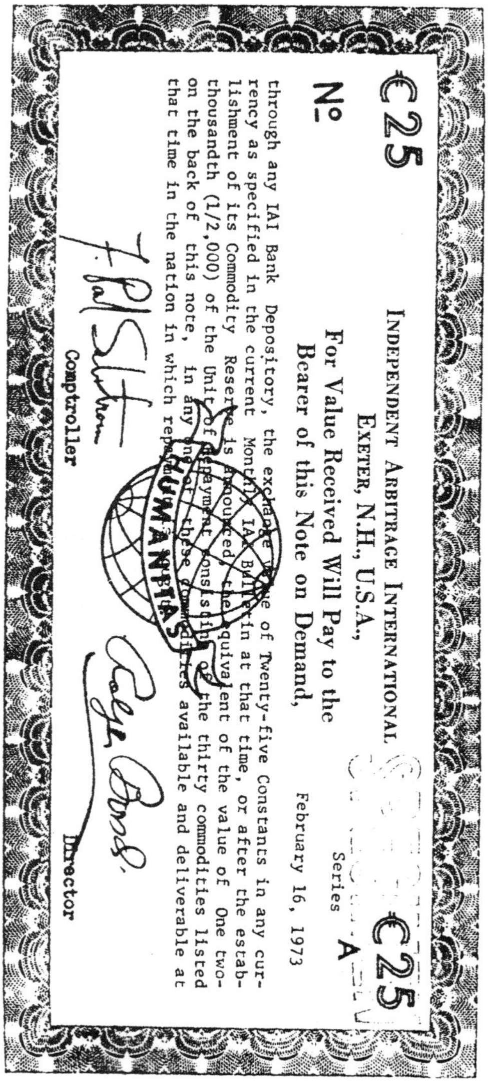

Figure 8.7: A *Constant* Note -- Face Side

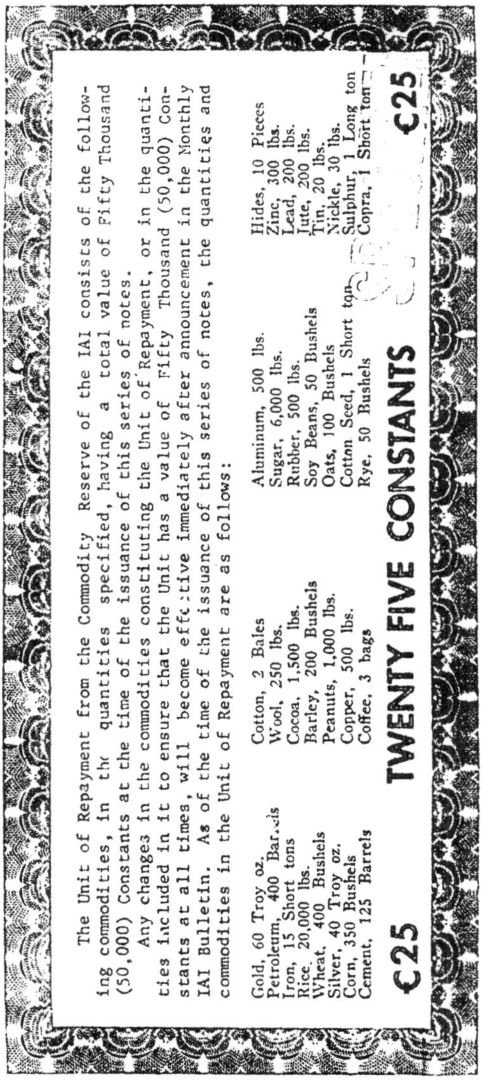

Figure 8.8: A *Constant* Note -- Reverse Side

An Early Proposal for a Credit Clearing System

As early as 1914, Bilgram and Levy proposed a "credit clearance" system.[49] They introduced their plan with the following statement:

> "Were a number of businessmen to combine for the purpose of organizing a system of exchange, effective among themselves, they could clearly demonstrate how simple the money system can really be made. The greater the number of businessmen that would thus cooperate, the more complete would be their own emancipation from the obstruction to commerce and industry which existing currency laws impose."

The plan which Bilgram and Levy outlined was basically as follows:

1. A group of businessmen would agree to settle their business accounts through a "clearing system," using their own credit as a medium of exchange.

2. The method of clearing accounts would be, in the main, similar to that used by depository banks to clear accounts among its depositors. Each businessmen's association would open an account for each of its members.

3. Each member would then furnish "thoroughly acceptable and amply adequate" security for the amount of credit he wished to establish.

4. The security would be held by the association as a pledge to cover the "credit cheques" which the member might draw in excess of his deposits, *i.e.* to secure his debit balance.

5. Such "credit cheques" would be accepted by all members of the association in payment of business accounts. The amount of the check would be credited to the payee's account (causing it to

---

[49] Bilgram and Levy, *op.cit.*, p. 416.

increase), and the same amount would be debited to the payer's account (causing it to decrease).

6. The Bilgram and Levy plan provided for official currency and checks to be deposited to the account also, with the stipulation that only system credits, not official money, could be paid out or withdrawn from the account.

7. Under this plan, members with net credits would be allowed to redeem a certain portion of them, say 20% each month, for official currency. This, of course, would require those with debits to provide the official currency for such redemptions.

8. Such associations in various localities could be federated to provide for interregional clearing of credits.

Most all businesses have accounts payable and accounts receivable. This plan provides a means of clearing the major part of these balances.

Mutual Credit and LETS systems are conceptually similar to Bilgram and Levy's Credit Clearance plan. Their plan, however, required that members deposit "security" in the form that conventional banks require, *i.e.* bonds, stocks, mortgages, etc.. Mutual Credit and LETS consider this to be an unnecessary burden, and require only the member's commitment to accept credits in payment. The rationale is that the privilege of continuing participation in the system will be sufficient inducement for members to honor their commitments. In the case of Mutual Credit systems, debit balances are limited to some amount determined by a member's trading volume, while LETS, as originally conceived, imposes no debit limits.

Further, neither Mutual Credit or LETS require debtors to deposit official money or allow creditors to withdraw official money, except that Mutual Credit, as conceived, requires a member upon withdrawing from the system, to clear any remaining debit balance with cash if s/he cannot deliver sufficient credits.

CHAPTER 9 GLOBAL FINANCE, INFLATION, AND LOCAL CURRENCIES

Future students of history will be shocked and angered by the fact that in 1945 the same monetary system that had driven the world to despair and disaster (in the 1930's), and had almost destroyed the civilization it was supposed to stand for, was revived on a much wider scope.

-- Jacques Rueff[50]

Why Central Governments and Central Banks Don't Like Local Currencies

A headline in a major daily newspaper reads, **Cash-Starved Argentine Provinces Turning Out Their Own Money** (see Figure 9.1).[51] The story tells of two remote provinces which were printing their own money in the form of small denomination provincial bonds (basically, IOUs of the provincial governments), and paying their employees with it. This "to the chagrin of national and international banking authorities."

But why should the national and international authorities (namely, the International Monetary Fund) be chagrined over provincial measures to provide their own exchange media? The stated reason, according to the article, is worry that the consequent expansion of the money supply would undermine the central government's efforts to reduce the inflation rate.

This may seem rather odd considering that it is central governments and central banks themselves which are the cause of inflation. Ralph Borsodi expressed this in no uncertain terms when he presented the following "facts":

> "1. The first is that inflation is *dishonest*. It is a form of embezzlement. What is worse, it is a form of legalized embezzlement. Those who ignore this fact in effect condone it. And there is no excuse whatever for condoning any form of stealing.

---

[50] Rueff, Jacques, *The Age of Inflation*, *op.cit.*, p. xii.

[51] *The Charlotte Observer*, Thursday, Nov. 28, 1985, Sec. A, p. 50.

50A THE CHARLOTTE OBSERVER Thursday, November 28, 1985

Cash-Starved Argentine Provinces Turning Out Their Own Money

By ANDRES OPPENHEIMER
Knight-Ridder Newspapers

MIAMI — Two remote Argentine provinces, short of cash to pay public employees, have come up with an easy solution.

They're printing their own money, to the chagrin of national and international banking authorities.

"We are paying all our public employees with provincial bonds," Roberto Romero, governor of the northern Argentina province of Salta, said in a telephone interview. He said Salta started printing its own IOUs because it wasn't getting federal currency fast enough.

"People can change these bonds for money at any bank," Romero said. "They can use them to shop at supermarkets and to buy cars or any other products."

The Argentine government is not smiling, and world bankers are worried that other cash-starved states will copy Salta's financial extravaganza and jeopardize Latin efforts to curb inflation and pay huge foreign debts.

The International Monetary Fund (IMF), the world's main financial inspector for debt-ridden countries, was concerned enough to bring up the issue in recent talks with the Argentine government, said sources in Argentina and Washington. The IMF does not comment on negotiations with individual countries.

After Salta started quietly issuing its IOUs in September last year, the nearby province of La Rioja started printing its own bonds, too. Four other Argentine provinces have either begun adopting similar programs or are preparing to do so.

In all cases, the bonds are good only within the province where they're issued.

But the government of President Raul Alfonsin says the provincial bonds are expanding the country's money supply and are undermining efforts to remove Argentina from the list of world inflation leaders. Earlier this year, Argentina had a 1,000% annual inflation rate.

Alfonsin made headlines worldwide in June when he launched an austerity program built around a commitment to stop his government from printing money. Since then, inflation has dropped to 3% a month, a record low in recent history.

The bonds printed in Salta come in denominations of 10, 100 and 1,000 australes, the same as ordinary Argentine currency bills. They pay no interest and can be either exchanged for Argentine currency or used to buy goods.

Romero, of the opposition Peronist party, and officials of other provinces claim their bonds are not really new currencies, because they are no good outside their provinces.

Figure 9.1: News Clip About Argentine Provincial Bonds

2. The second fact is that the inflation is *deliberate*. It was planned. It is in actuality a sort of conspiracy entered into by nations and those who represented and participated in the International Monetary Conference held in Bretton Woods, New Hampshire in 1944. It is an on-going conspiracy still being carried out by all the nations which are members of the International Monetary Fund. The dishonesty involved is therefore deliberate.

3. The third is that it is *unnecessary*. None of the so-called reasons, none of the excuses and rationalizations of those who are responsible for inflation or who condone or justify it, have any real validity.

4. The fourth and final fact is that almost without exception those leaders of the world who say they are against inflation and claim to be fighting against it, are *lying*. It is a lie to say that you are against something which you are in truth advocating. It is a lie to say that you are against something which you are in fact deliberately doing. It is a lie to advocate doing a little of what in fact should not be done at all. It is a lie to say you are against stealing , when you are in fact saying that a little stealing is alright. It is a lie to say that a little inflation, say two or three percent, is not stealing, but that a lot of inflation, say ten or twenty or thirty percent, is all wrong."[52]

This story about the Argentine provincial bonds is another instance of the conflict between exploiter and exploited. We see, on the one hand, the central government, supported by the international financial hierarchy, attempting to maintain its control over the entire national economy via its control over money creation and circulation. We see, on the other hand, the provincial authorities implementing measures to ameliorate the effects of central government and central bank policies which have been damaging to their local economies. By supplementing scarce official money with their own money issues, the provincial governments counter the stifling effects of the central government's and central bank's policies. These policies include alternating monetary expansion and

---

[52] Borsodi, *Inflation and the Coming Keynesian Catastrophe*, *op.cit.*, pp. 6-7.

contraction, mis-allocation of credit to finance privilege and to increase central power, and domestic "austerity" imposed upon the people to pay for it.

The Real Cause of Inflation

In order to understand the exploitative nature of centralized monetary control, it is first necessary to understand what inflation is, and what really causes it. Much of the problem of understanding inflation stems from the confused definition which economists use. A dictionary definition provides a good illustration of this confusion. Here is what it says: "Inflation 2.*Economics*. An abnormal increase in available currency and credit beyond the proportion of available goods, resulting in a sharp and continuing rise in price levels."[53]

In this definition we see the conventional "wisdom" reflected. We see a presumed cause, "an abnormal increase in available currency and credit," coupled with an observed effect, "a sharp and continuing rise in price levels." But this presumption stands upon shaky ground. It is more apparent than real. Let us hold in abeyance the question of cause, and define inflation as the effect -- a rise in the general level of prices of goods and services -- for this is the essence of the problem.

Since the price of something is an expression of its value relative to the money being used to value it, an increase can result in two ways. First, it can be due to people valuing the item more, or secondly, it can be due to people valuing the money less. Conditions of supply and demand can cause price adjustments of particular goods or commodities. But when the prices of most goods and services are rising simultaneously, that invariably reflects a debasement of the currency in terms of which the prices are stated. Sellers demand more money because each unit of money is worth less than it was before.

---

[53] *American Heritage Dictionary*. New York: American Heritage Publishing Co., 1973.

So to summarize, inflation is a rise in the general level of prices of goods and services, and its cause is the debasement of the official currency. Few economists seem willing to acknowledge official debasement as the root cause of inflation. Fewer still offer any effective remedy. Most orthodox proposals seek only to limit the rate of debasement, not to end it.

It is not the amount of money in circulation, per se, which causes inflation, but the basis upon which the money is issued. Money which is improperly issued can be viewed as counterfeit, albeit legal counterfeit. It is counterfeit, not because its issuance is unauthorized, but because its issuance violates sound principles of money and banking. The mixture of such counterfeit money with legitimate money, since they are indistinguishable from one another, causes the debasement of the entire money supply.

We have already seen how the issuance of money on the basis of interest-bearing debt causes a chronic insufficiency of money in general circulation. The primary cause of inflation is the issuance of money on the basis of ever increasing and unrepayable debt, primarily that of central governments (to finance perpetual budget deficits). This is called "monetizing the debt." It is an abuse of power which is almost universal among governments in the modern world.[54]

Other improper bases of issue include capital investments, such as tools and machinery; speculation in land, real estate, stocks, and other securities; and consumer credit. Surely, capital investments, construction, and consumer durables need to be financed, but they ought to be

---

[54] In some countries the government issues money directly (through the central bank which it controls) by spending it into circulation. In the United States, the federal government does not issue money directly. It is the Federal Reserve, a private banking cartel, which issues U.S. money, as bank credit or in the form of Federal Reserve notes. The Federal Reserve is not under the control of the government. Indeed, it can be reasonably argued that it is the other way around. But the evidence shows that the Federal Reserve will do whatever is necessary to accommodate any level of government spending, no matter how profligate.

financed out of savings of money already in existence. New money which is created on the basis of anything except the exchange of goods and services coming to market represents a debasement of the currency and will cause inflation of prices in the market.[55]

The irresponsible and unsound banking practices which give rise to inflation can be compared to a farmer watering his milk. The farmer who takes his milk bucket to the well can increase the volume of fluid (milk mixed with water) but the volume of real milk remains the same. The total amount of nutrients in the bucket does not change. If the farmer tries to sell the mixture as pure milk he is defrauding his customers.

Real value comes from the efforts of producers, not from debt which is never intended to be repaid. Money issued to finance goods, in or on the way to market, is legitimate; it represents the milk of the economy. Money issued to finance the government debt is valueless; it is like water, diluting the value of every legitimate dollar in circulation. It allows the government to take more value from the economy than it ever will put into it. It is for this reason that inflation has been called a "hidden tax."

It is astonishing that even the most respected economists still prescribe "massive government spending" as the medicine required to end an economic recession. Implicit in this prescription is the intention that this massive spending will be financed, not out of increased tax revenues, but by the creation of new money. This is like telling the farmer that the way to end the malnutrition of his customers is to add still more water to his milk.

To completely understand the monetary problem, we should look not only at inflation, but also at its opposite, deflation. The dictionary

---

[55] This subject of the proper basis of issue is addressed more completely in Appendix B, which contains excerpts from "The Lost Art of Commercial Banking" by E. C. Harwood, taken from *How Safe Is Your Bank*, published by the American Institute for Economic Research, Great Barrington, MA 01230, 1989.

definition is: "Deflation 2. *Economics.* A reduction in the general price level, brought on by a decrease in the amount of money in circulation or by a decrease in the total volume of spending."[56] This time the dictionary correctly defines deflation as, "a reduction in the general price level," but the definition again includes a presumed relationship with the amount of money in circulation.

But again, it is not just a matter of the amount of money in circulation; it is more a matter of banks not lending for things they should. When banks lend for purposes they should not, while neglecting to lend for purposes they should, the result is simultaneous inflation of prices due to debasement of the currency, along with decline of economic activity (recession) due to inadequate amounts of money being issued to the private sector for productive purposes.

Given a choice between inflation and deflation, inflation is considered by many to be the lesser of evils. But that depends upon your point of view and the source from which you derive your livelihood. When there is more money sloshing around (even if some of it is counterfeit), the little guy may be more likely to get a bit of it from within the private sector. On the other hand, when banks are failing to lend enough new money into the productive sector in a mistaken attempt to control inflation, they bring about defaults and bankruptcies, which, in turn, cause greater unemployment. Thus, many people are cut off completely, while those who are able to maintain some source of income fare well because of falling prices.[57]

---

[56] *American Heritage Dictionary, op.cit.*

[57] Another means of keeping the prices of basic commodities low is by use of military intervention or threat of intervention to keep weaker countries from restricting or closing-off access to raw materials and export products. Thus, the Gulf War of 1991, the CIA engineered coup in Chile, and innumerable interventions around the world by the U.S. government made it possible for the U.S. to "export its inflation" to a large extent. The so-called free trade agreements like NAFTA, and the GATT, are diplomatic attempts to do the same thing.

Those who lose their jobs, farms, or businesses can only hope for direct government payments in the form of welfare and unemployment benefits. In either case, when government appropriates more of the nation's wealth by deficit spending, it is able to dictate the direction of economic activity. Greater numbers of citizens are required to do its bidding, either in the military, as employees in the government's bureaucracy, or by working for its corporate and academic minions (engaging in such activities as designing and building weapons, space and scientific boondoggles, and infrastructure development to benefit favored interests). Others, who lack the requisite skills, have little choice but to suffer the indignities of being "on the dole." The central economic planning for which socialist and communist countries have been so roundly criticized has, unfortunately, become the modus operandi of the "capitalist" west.

To sum up then, when the government covertly takes value out of the economy (which is evident from budget deficits and ever-increasing government debt), the people pay for it in either of two ways --recession or inflation. In a recession, some people are deprived of their share of the total product as a result of losing their jobs, their businesses, or their homes, or having social programs cut. When the debasement of money causes inflation, the dollars people get don't buy as much as they did before.

A recession is like the farmer refusing to deliver milk to some of his customers, even though they have already paid for it, so he can keep more milk for himself. Currency debasement is like the farmer adding water to the remaining quantity of milk so that, while he may continue to deliver the same amount of liquid to each of his customers, that inferior liquid (milk mixed with water) will provide them less nourishment and satisfaction.

Of course, it is possible for governments and central banks to use both strategies simultaneously, doing some of each. It has long been recognized that the existing economic structure requires a trade-off between unemployment and inflation, and public policy decisions have made this a primary focus. But economists are still scratching their heads trying to explain the more recent experience of simultaneous inflation and recession.

With that foundation laid, let us return to our story of the Argentinean provincial currencies. More up-to-date information has become available through an article by Argentine native Jose' Reissig which appeared in the English journal, *New Economics*.[58]

The province of Salta, in 1985, was the first Argentinean province to issue bonds in small denominations and to spend them into circulation. One such bond in the denomination of 100 Australes is shown in Figure 9.2. By 1986, according to Reissig's article, three neighboring provinces, La Rioja, Jujuy, and Tucuman, had followed Salta's lead in issuing bonds into circulation. As of the end of 1991, they remained in circulation and comprised an important component of the money supply in those regions. "The bonds have become an intrinsic feature of the economy of Salta. Today they are more in evidence than the national australes, amounting perhaps to 60 percent of all currency in circulation."[59] Reissig further states that in the province of Tucaman, provincial bonds at that time provided about 43 percent of the exchange media.

It may seem surprising to find that these bonds were still circulating, and that the central government had not been willing (or able) to suppress them. Reissig speculates that it may be simply because the provincial bonds, while providing a large portion of the exchange media in the provinces that issued them, constitute a relatively insignificant portion of the total money supply nationally.

This case provides an opportunity to consider two of the critical questions which relate to local currencies. First is the question of what happens to a local currency which is denominated in the same units as the national currency which is being debased (causing inflation)? A second question is, what are the factors which make a local currency credible enough to be accepted? Let's consider these in turn.

---

[58] "Bonds That Brought a Boom" by Jose' Reissig, in *New Economics*, #20, Winter 1991, London, England.

[59] *ibid.*

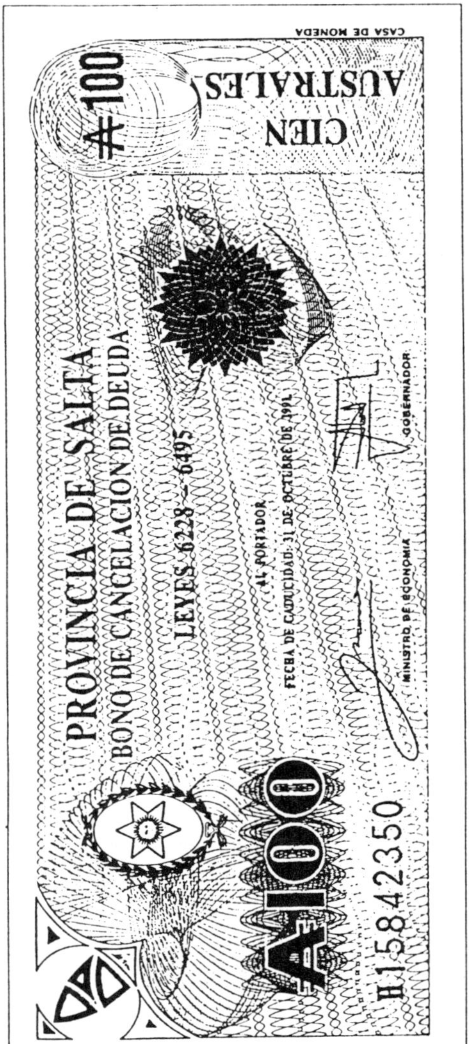

Figure 9.2: A Circulating Bond of Salta Province

The bonds were denominated in terms of the official unit of account, which was the official currency unit, the "austral."[60] They typically mature in about four years from the time of issuance. As the official currency is debased (inflated), the official unit of account loses more of its value. Since the provincial bonds are denominated in the official units, they will also depreciate along with the official currency. At the inflation rates typical of the recent past in Argentina (ranging from 95 percent to several hundred percent per year, except for a couple brief periods of stability), this is enough to make the bonds almost worthless in terms of purchasing power over the period of their maturity. This factor is taken into account by those accepting them. As with the official currency, no one intends to hold onto them for very long.

As Reissig says, "The bonds make it possible for the provincial government to share in the revenues of the inflationary tax." That is true enough, but it is clearly not the primary intention of a provincial government in issuing them. The dependence upon an exchange medium which must be imported from outside the region (official currency), makes the local economy dependent, to a large extent, upon the central government and/or central bank. In order to acquire official money, it must subordinate regional priorities to the demands of the central government in order to obtain a share of government spending, or it must compete for loans from the banking system, or it must earn official currency by exporting products and services out of the region. If local needs are to take first priority in the local economy, the local economy must be able of itself to mediate internal exchanges; it can do this only by using an exchange medium which is not controlled by outside agencies.

According to Reissig, a native Argentinean, prices in that country are now widely quoted in terms of U.S. dollars, and "many firms are doing their accounting in U.S. units." While the U.S. dollar has also been subject to debasement (inflation), it has provided a relatively stable unit

---

[60] I have information from Mr. Reissig that on January 1, 1992, "four zeros were dropped from the national currency, which was renamed the peso instead of austral." From personal correspondence dated March 10, 1992.

of account compared to the *austral* and the currencies of other less developed countries.

As for the factors which may provide credibility and acceptability of the provincial bonds, Reissig mentions the following:

1. The time factor -- the provincial government was willing to pay its employees in either its provincial bonds or official Argentine currency; however, they could receive the bonds immediately, while they would have to wait a few days for the official currency.

2. The provincial bonds could be exchanged at the local banks for official currency at par.

3. For a period of time the provincial government used the bonds as the basis for a lottery, making the bonds serve also as lottery tickets (the lottery was discontinued in 1987).

4. People in the region soon realized that the circulation of a limited, local currency had the effect of stimulating local businesses.

5. The provincial government agreed to accept its bonds in payment for provincial taxes and services.

6. The Chamber of Commerce agreed to accept the bonds.[61]

It is possible that the provincial authorities might also abuse their power by over-issuing bonds, but they would pay a high price in doing so. Since there is no forced circulation of the bonds, and since they must compete in the market with the official currency, over-issuance would cause the bonds to trade below par relative to the *austral*. This would cause a loss of revenue for the provincial government, since they would still have to redeem the bonds at par. According to Reissig, there has been some abuse of this sort in the province of Salta. During one period in 1987, the Salta bonds were being discounted by as much as 20% with

[61] Personal correspondence dated April 20, 1992.

respect to the official Argentine currency. This situation was remedied, as one might expect, by a temporary suspension or slowing down the rate of issuance of the bonds.[62]

Recent information from Argentina indicates that the provincial government of Salta was planning, as of March 31, 1992, to redeem its bonds for official currency, using a loan obtained from the central government. Just prior to this time the bonds were again being debased as indicated by the fact that they were being traded at an approximately 15% discount from the official currency. It is not known whether the other provinces were planning to follow suit in calling in their bonds.[63] One can only speculate as to the reasons for this action, but it is not too far-fetched to consider that it might be related to the results of the 1991 elections and the provinces' changing relationships with the central government.

---

[62] *ibid.*

[63] *ibid.*

CHAPTER 10 CURRENT EXAMPLES OF LOCAL CURRENCY AND CASHLESS EXCHANGE

"I like the idea of local people putting money directly into each others' pockets. Big industry is nothing to depend on; they're closing down and moving out. I prefer to support people I know and trust."

-- Jenny[64]

Barter, Reciprocal Trade, and Mutual Credit

In recent years there has been a proliferation of so-called "Barter" clubs and exchanges, including both non-profit clubs which serve individuals and communities, and commercial exchanges established to service business clients. For the most part, the activities of these groups do not involve barter transactions at all, but rather some form of what has come to be known as "reciprocal trade."

In common usage, the word "barter" is frequently used to describe any exchange that does not utilize official money, but this is grossly inaccurate. A barter transaction involves only two parties, each of whom has something the other wants. When party A gives item X to party B, and receives item Y from party B in return, then a complete barter transaction has taken place. If, however, one of the parties has nothing desired by the other, there can be no barter transaction. The primary role of money is to transcend the barter limitation by serving as an intermediary exchange medium.

But something other than official money may be offered as an intermediary. This can be a personal IOU which must be "made good" at some later time. More commonly, the intermediary will be a generalized IOU which a group of associated traders have agreed to honor. Such arrangements are more accurately referred to as "reciprocal trade" or "mutual credit." The distinction between reciprocal trade and mutual credit will be explained in a later chapter.

---

[64] *Ithaca Money*, No. 14, December 1993-January, 1994.

Commercial "Barter" Exchanges

"Barter" or reciprocal trade has become big business in North America, and I presume, in other parts of the industrialized world as well. There are presently in the U.S. alone, several hundred "barter" or trade exchanges. These exchanges generally operate as private incorporated businesses which collectively cater to the needs of hundred of thousands of clients, mostly small and medium sized businesses, but including many large, well-known companies. Billions of dollars of sales are mediated each year by commercial exchanges[65].

A trade association known as the International Reciprocal Trade Association, or IRTA, was founded in 1979 "to foster the common interests of the commercial barter industry in the United States and worldwide, and to uphold high standards of ethical business practice."[66]

According to IRTA, the rapid expansion of the barter industry is due to several factors, including:

1. The availability of computers which facilitate the accounting and tracking of barter transactions.

2. The growing appeal of cashless trading among business owners and professionals because it allows them to:
   a. generate extra sales, thus reducing unit costs,
   b. open up new outlets for disposing of excess inventory,
   c. conserve their cash for essential expenditures.[67]

How Trade Exchanges Operate

Barter exchanges generally charge their members several hundred dollars to join, plus an annual membership fee. In addition, they charge a

---

[65] IRTA Fact Sheet, *The Commercial Barter Industry.*

[66] IRTA Fact Sheet, *The International Reciprocal Trade Association.*

[67] *The Commercial Barter Industry, op.cit.*

commission, often 10% to 15%, on the gross value of each transaction. Membership fees are generally payable in official currency, but commissions may be payable in trade credits.

Trade exchanges perform two basic functions for their members. They act first of all as a clearing house, keeping accounts of members' transactions and trade balances, and secondly, they actively stimulate trading by brokering merchandise, either finding buyers for members' merchandise or buying it for their own account for later sale.

The contract between the trade exchange and its members specifies the respective responsibilities of each party. As part of the agreement, trade dollars are issued by a trade exchange by making loans to its members. Each member will have a particular "line of credit" (in trade dollars) which defines the maximum negative (debit) balance which that member is allowed to carry. Thus, a trade or "barter" exchange, in effect, issues its own currency, not in the form of circulating notes, but as accounting debits and credits. The amount loaned to each member must, of course, be based upon the credit-worthiness of that member, which is largely dependent upon the demand for his goods or services. This process is very similar to the way in which banks create conventional money.

The accounting unit used in exchange transactions is the "trade dollar." When a member sells services of merchandise to another member, his account is credited for the fair market value, in dollars, of the merchandise, while the buying member's account is debited (reduced) by a corresponding amount, not considering commission charges levied by the trade exchange.

In general, trade exchange operators have the power to borrow trade credits for their own account. In the past, some trade exchange operators have abused this power, spending credits in amounts well beyond their capacity to earn them through fees. As a result, the willingness of their members to sell merchandise and services for trade credits has declined, trade credits have lost their value, and the exchanges have failed. IRTA has assumed a self-regulatory function to try to alleviate such abuses and protect the industry.

Tax Implications of Commercial Barter Trade

Barter exchange members are required to provide the exchange with their taxpayer identification number (TIN). In accordance with the Tax Equity Act of 1982, all barter transactions are recorded and the barter income of each client is reported to the IRS for tax purposes at the end of each year (using form 1099B). Income received in the form of trade credits is considered by the IRS to be taxable.

> "Each barter taxpayer must include in gross income the amount of his barter income. However, the taxpayer is entitled to include barter purchases made for business purposes with his cash deductions for business expenses."[68]

LETS -- Local Employment and Trading System

LETS is an acronym which originally derived from "Local Exchange Trading System," but eventually became "Local Employment and Trading System." It is probably the best working example of a type of system which can be generically referred to as "Mutual Credit" or "Community Credit."[69] LETS was originated by Michael Linton of British Columbia, Canada, in the early 1980's. Since then, LETS systems have proliferated around the world. There are now literally hundreds of active LETS systems in various stages of development in many countries, mainly in the English-speaking world. As of late 1993, there were about 10 LETS systems in the U.S., 20 in Canada, 20 in Ireland, 120 in Britain, 60 in New Zealand, and 160 in Australia.

Recognizing the limitations and dysfunctions of the dominant national currency systems, Linton devised an approach to facilitating trade

---

[68] Suplizio, Paul E., *Commercial Barter Exchanges in Society*, an address presented to the Chicago Association of Commerce and Industry, Chicago, September 18, 1985, IRTA, 1985.

[69] See also, the description of LETS which appeared in an illustrated article entitled, "The Local Employment and Trading System", by Michael Linton and Thomas Greco, in *Whole Earth Review*, No. 55, Summer 1987.

without the need for scarce official money. He realized that the fundamental characteristic of money, which allows it to facilitate exchange, is the information which it carries. He envisioned another information system which would be locally controlled and operated in parallel with the official monetary system. He designed LETS as a not-for-profit association run by and for its members. It was never intended to replace the official currency, but only to supplement it. By its nature, LETS is limited, local, and personal, and it is these characteristics which give it its strength.

A LETS system operates very much like a commercial "barter" system but it has several notable differences in philosophy, intent, and practice:

1. LETS is a not-for-profit cooperative arrangement, usually unincorporated and operated by volunteers, whereas commercial "barter" exchanges are for-profit businesses.
2. LETS caters to individual traders, although business members are also welcome and desired, while commercial exchanges favor large volume business clients.
3. In LETS, the initiation and membership fees are nominal, sufficient only to cover the modest operating expenses of the system. Commercial exchanges charge large cash fees for membership and take a substantial percentage, usually in cash, on each transaction.
4. In LETS, there is generally no interest charged on either debit or credit balances.
5. While commercial exchanges actively broker trades among their members, LETS functions only as a clearinghouse and information service; there is generally no brokering of goods or services by LETS itself.[70]

Since LETS is a membership organization, LETS credits can be spent only within the membership group. This stimulates the local LETS member group to produce for its own needs and to import less from outside. Reducing imports from outside reduces the need to earn official

---

[70] This may be a shortcoming of LETS groups. The help of a "broker" to stimulate trading might enhance the usefulness of LETS for many members. Brokers might take a commission in LETS credits.

currency. Because it is small and personal, LETS also builds community and encourages members to support one another in a variety of ways.

LETS systems typically consist of a set of accounts, usually kept on a personal computer.[71] A LETS system is like a bank in that each member has an account to which transactions are credited or debited. Like a checking account, your LETS account is credited (increased, +) when you sell something and debited (reduced, -) when you buy something. The two parties to the trade negotiate the price as they ordinarily would for a cash transaction, but, instead of using cash, the seller receives credits and the buyer is "charged" a corresponding amount as a debit.

The unit of account in the original LETS system is the "green dollar," and LETS credits are often refer to simply as "green," but each local LETS system, being independent, is free to choose any name it wants for its accounting unit. Since we are all accustomed to evaluating things in terms of the official currency, LETS uses that same value concept (dollars in the U.S., pounds in Britain, etc.) for accounting. Thus, members tend to equate the value of a "green dollar" with the value of a Federal Reserve dollar in the United States, or a Bank of Canada dollar in Canada. Unlike official dollar bank credits or cash, however, which can only be created by the banking system, LETS dollars or green dollar credits are created by LETS members themselves as needed to execute a trade. This is the crucial element which makes LETS and other mutual credit systems so empowering.

Every account begins with a balance of zero. Sales of goods or services add to one's account balance, while purchases reduce one's balance. Account balances may be negative and normally there is no interest charged on balances, though the members may agree to limit the amount of debit which a member may carry. A member with a negative or debit balance, however, is "committed" to supply that much value to others in

---

[71] The members of a few LETS systems are presently considering supplementing their ledger systems with paper "receipts", which would function like paper currency, providing all the convenience and advantages of a circulating currency.

the system at some time in the future. Having a negative balance in a LETS system is not a problem. In fact, positive balances can only exist if there are negative balances. The total of positive balances in a LETS system is always equal to the total of negative balances. Besides not charging interest on balances, there is no repayment schedule for debit balances in a LETS system. There is, however, the expectation that members with debit balances will actively offer their services to prevent their accounts being permanently in debit. Members' balances are not secret but may be made known to any other member upon request. Some LETS systems routinely publish all account balances periodically to give members a sense of the state of the system. It is still a matter of debate as to whether the published list of account balances should include members' names.

Transactions are reported to the LETS registrar or record keeper either by telephone or mail. Account balances are updated periodically and each member is sent a statement of account showing his/her transactions for the period, and his/her beginning and ending balances. In addition to the account statement, members usually receive a "noticeboard" or listing of goods and services being offered and requested. This noticeboard is actually a form of classified advertising by which members can advertise what they want and what they have to sell. Some LETS groups also publish a directory which gives more details about each members' interests, skills and needs.

As with any system, there are costs involved in the operation of LETS. Some of these are cash costs for such things as copying, postage, telephone service, etc. These are usually covered by charging an annual membership fee, and/or set-up fee in cash. Other costs, such as record-keeping, publication, management, and other services provided by LETS members are typically paid in LETS credits. These are covered by charging members, in LETS credits or green dollars, for recording transactions, printing account statements, and noticeboard advertising.

How Does LETS Work?

To illustrate how LETS works, let's trace the steps which one might take from becoming a member to receiving her/his first statement of account.

Suppose Amy wishes to join LETS-Happyville. She fills out a membership agreement and pays an initial set-up fee of $5, plus her first year's membership fee of $15. She is given a copy of the current noticeboard and directory and an instruction sheet telling how to report transactions, as well as other system procedures. Amy's account balance begins at zero.

Amy sees from the noticeboard listings that Sarah is offering automobile tune-ups, and that John is offering deep massage and acupressure treatments. She also notes that Harold wants fresh-baked, whole-wheat bread and fresh vegetables. Amy sees in each of these a potential trade. She negotiates with Sarah to have her car tuned up. They agree on a price of 30 green dollars, plus $20 in cash to cover the cost of ignition points and spark plugs. She also negotiates with John to get two acupressure treatments for a total of 40 green dollars plus $10 cash. Next, Amy sells to Harold 2 loaves of her fresh-baked bread for 5 green dollars; she also sells him an assortment of vegetables from her garden for 10 green dollars.

The cash portion of the transactions is handled by the parties to the trades. Only the green dollar amounts are reported to the LETS registrar. On the tune-up, Amy is debited 30, on the acupressure treatments she is debited 40, and on her sales to Harold she is credited 15. If this is the extent of her trading for the period, her account statement at the end of the period will show a negative or debit balance of 55 green dollars (-30 -40 + 15). There might also be system charges (additional debits) of 2 green dollars for her own noticeboard advertising and statement fee, making her ending balance a minus 57. Meanwhile, Sarah's account has been credited 30, John's has been credited 40 and Harold's has been debited 15.

There is no particular time within which Amy must clear her debit balance. She understands, however, that her debit represents her promise to the community of members. She will, in all probability, try to keep her debit balance from becoming chronic or excessive. A primary reason for making account balances public within the system is to encourage self-regulation. In such a situation, a member with a chronic or excessive debit balance may find it increasingly more difficult to find members willing to sell to her/him. By using the LETS system, Amy has "saved" $55 of hard-to-get cash on services that she needed, she has employed her friends and neighbors, and has, in effect, employed herself by providing others with the means to purchase her own goods and services.[72]

Figure 10.1, shows the creation and circulation of LETS credits. The LETS credit trading circuit conforms closely to the ideal money circuit described in Chapter 2. As in the ideal money circuit, Mr. Able creates a LETS credit when he buys something from Mr. Baker. Baker, in turn, uses it to buy something from Mr. Cook. The credit continues to circulate around until Ms. Zane uses it to buy something from Mr. Able who created it in the first place. When Mr. Able accepts it, the credit has returned to its source and ceases to exist. Of course Mr. Able can begin the process anew by buying something else for LETS credits which he can create just as he did before. Any other LETS member can do the same.

LETS In Operation

Since Michael Linton introduced it in 1983, LETS has attracted considerable attention and local systems have sprung up around the world. Articles about it have appeared in magazines and major daily newspapers, and LETS has been featured on national television programs in several countries.

While LETS in the U.S. and Canada has been only a modest success, it has really taken off in other parts of the English-speaking world, notably Britain, Australia and New Zealand. The numbers of local LETS systems operating in Britain and Australia seem to be growing exponentially. New Zealand's 60 or so exchanges have thus far mediated trades worth hundreds of thousands of dollars. Its Auckland LETS system is, perhaps, the largest anywhere with over 2,000

---

[72] Detailed information about how to start and operate a LETS system can be obtained from sources indicated in the section headed, *Sources and Resources*. This section also contains a list of selected operating LETSystems and software sources.

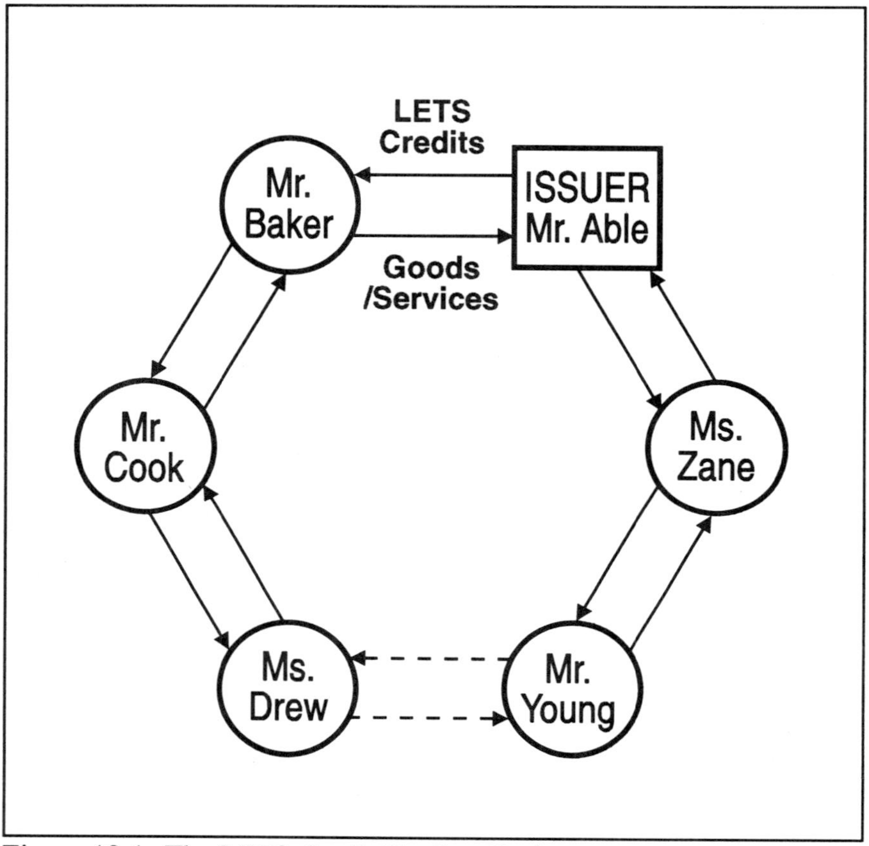

Figure 10.1: The LETS Credit Trading Cycle

members.[73] Australia has more LETS systems than any other country, 160 at last count, the largest being the Blue Mountains LETS near Sidney, with over 1000 members. A nationwide Australian conference in 1992 attracted 70 participants representing 40 different LETS systems.

---

[73] Ruth Hobson, "The Amazing Growth of LETS in the UK", in *LETSlink Newsletter*, May 1993.

The government of the province of Western Australia has allocated \$A50,000 to help launch new LETS systems in that region.[74]

In Britain, a national coordinating body called LETSLink has been established to help coordinate LETS activity and support the establishment of new systems. LETSLink has received favorable media attention which has prompted inquiries from Europe, Africa and Asia. A television documentary is being prepared for release in early 1994.[75]

In Canada, the number of LETS systems continues to grow. The Toronto LETSystem has reached a membership of over 300, and reports trading of over \$200,000 since start-up.[76]

It isn't entirely clear why LETS has flourished in these other countries while languishing in the U.S. It may be that the need is greater there, and perhaps the economic and social climates are more favorable than in North America. Differing attitudes and relationships with the various taxing authorities also seem to be a factor. It seems certain, however, that as the conventional national economies continue to decline and more people become marginalized, mutual credit and local currency systems will become increasingly popular and important to the restoration of sound regional economies.

The Berkshire Experiments

A group in Massachusetts, known as SHARE (Self-help Association for a Regional Economy) has recently managed to instigate some successful local currency experiments. These have gotten quite a bit of media attention, including reports on national network television and a major article in the Washington Post, in addition to coverage in local newspapers. These experiments have consisted of at least four local

---

[74] *ibid*, and conversations with Michael Linton in September of 1993.

[75] *K-W LETSLetter*, #16, September 1993, p.2.

[76] *ibid*.

currency issues -- Berkshire Farm Preserve Notes, Deli Dollars, Monterey General Store scrip and Kintaro Restaurant scrip.[77]

Each of these scrip issues has been of the same type, functioning much like gift certificates. The certificates are sold for cash, usually at a small discount, and redeemed in trade by the issuing businesses sometime later. In the meantime, they can be circulated from hand to hand as money, though there is little information available regarding the extent to which this has happened.

These experiments have been very limited in their scope, and these scrip issues, by their nature, have not provided a medium for general circulation. They have, however, been enthusiastically accepted and supported by the local community, proving the practicability of local currencies. The Farm Preserve Notes, furthermore, have received official sanction by the Massachusetts State Agriculture Department which is eager to support the state's few remaining farms. The main effect of such notes has been to provide the issuers with working capital in the off-season.

SHARE is currently working on the development of a more comprehensive scrip issue, called the "Berkshare," which will not be sold for dollars, but will be spent into circulation by members of a consortium of local businesses, each on the basis of its capacity to provide value to the community. Figures 10.2 and 10.3, respectively, show a Deli Dollar and a Massachusetts Farmer's Market Coupon.

Ithaca HOURS

To my knowledge, the most successful present-day local currency plan in the United States is the *Ithaca HOUR* initiated by Paul Glover in Ithaca, New York. Since the project was launched in November of 1991, there has been rapid growth in both the number of traders using the local currency and the volume of trading. As of October, 1993,

---

[77] See *The Washington Post*, Monday, May 20, 1991, Section A, page 1. This article describes *Deli Dollars* and *Berkshire Farm Preserve Notes*. See also, *The Berkshire Record*, April 26, 1991, Section B, page 1, which describes all four scrip issues.

Figure 10.2: A Deli Dollar $10 Note

4,200 *HOURS* (equivalent to about $42,000) had been issued into circulation, and the number of participants accepting *HOURS* in trade has increased to about 800. Glover claims that several hundred thousand

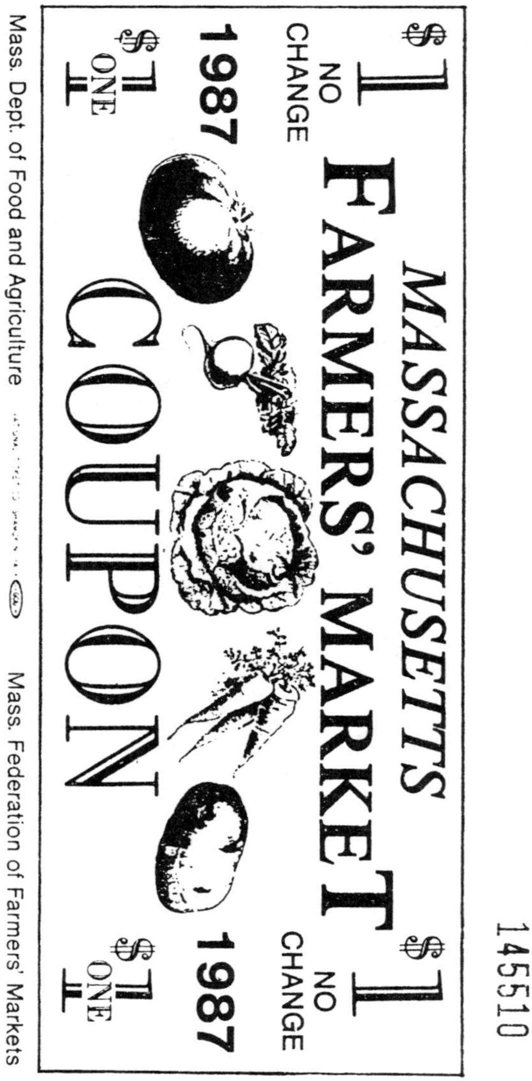

Figure 10.3: A Massachusetts Farmer's Market Coupon

Figure 10.4: An *Ithaca HOUR* 1 Hour Note -- Face Side

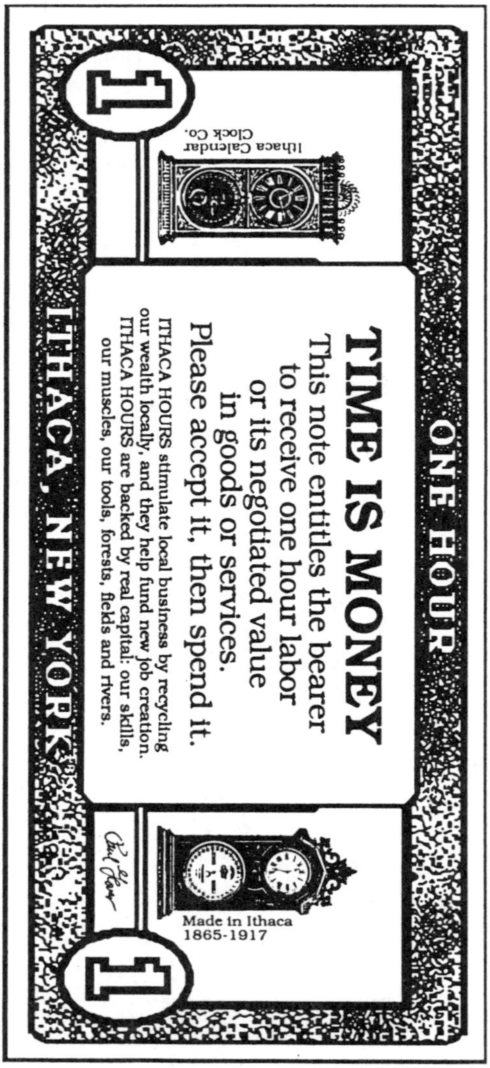

Figure 10.5: An *Ithaca HOUR* 1 Hour Note -- Reverse Side

dollars of trading has been facilitated by *Ithaca HOURS* since the plan was launched.[78] *Ithaca HOUR* notes have been issued in denominations of 1/4, 1/2, 1, and 2 hours. The two sides of the 1 hour denomination is shown in Figures 10.4 and 10.5.

Ithaca HOURS have begun to attract a considerable amount of attention. It was the subject of the cover article in a recent issue of Mother Earth News (#139, Aug./Sept., 1993), and was featured in a major Japanese television broadcast seen by an estimated 35 million viewers.[79]

The foundation for the plan is a two-color tabloid newspaper called *Ithaca MONEY*, which Glover publishes and distributes free of charge. The newspaper contains information about the local economy, community self-help initiatives, and the benefits of local currencies, but its primary purpose is to publicize the individuals and businesses which have agreed to accept the local currency in payment for their goods and services. Each issue of the newspaper contains classified-type listings of both offers and requests for goods and services, as well as display ads. Ads can be paid for either in dollars or *HOURS*.

The means of issuance of *HOURS* is very simple. Each advertiser who agrees to accept *HOURS* in either full or partial payment, is issued notes worth 4 *HOURS* <u>as a premium</u> for his/her participation. They are then free to spend their *HOURS* on purchases from anyone willing to accept them; the seller need not be an Ithaca Money advertiser. *Ithaca MONEY* issues an additional 2 *HOURS* to those whose goods or services have been listed in four issues. Those who sign-up or renew at one of the monthly Barter Potlucks are paid a bonus of one *HOUR*.

Glover does not claim to be the issuer of a local currency but merely the publisher of a newspaper. The *HOUR* notes which advertisers receive have no foundation other than the agreement of his advertisers to accept them in trade. Decisions regarding operations are made collectively on

---

[78] *Ithaca Money*, No. 13, October-November, 1993.

[79] *ibid.*

an ad hoc basis by those who attend the monthly "Barter Potlucks" which are an informal adjunct to the publication of the newspaper.

The Ithaca HOUR plan includes a novel form of "tithing." Barter Potlucks have decided to support community organizations by making grants of *HOURS* which they can then spend for needed goods and services. The current policy provides that about 10% of all *HOURS* issued go into circulation as grants to local organizations. The allocation of *HOUR* grants among the organizational applicants is made by those attending each month's Barter Potluck. So far, grants have been made to 21 different organizations.

Besides the dedication and energy of its founder, the success of the *Ithaca HOUR* plan can probably be attributed mainly to its elegant simplicity. Other probable contributing factors are Ithaca's small size, its remoteness from any large city, and its highly educated and progressive population.

Ithaca MONEY has also begun offering a "Home Town Money Starter Kit" for $25 or 2 1/2 *Ithaca HOURS*. The kit includes "all start-up and maintenance procedures, forms, laws, news articles, computer programs, updates and an *Ithaca MONEY* subscription." As of late 1993, over 150 kits had been distributed to people in 39 states. See the *Sources and Resources* section for the address.

Boulder HOURS

One area in which the Ithaca influence has taken hold is Boulder, Colorado. Patterned after the Ithaca model, *Boulder HOURS* were put into circulation beginning in mid-1993. *HOURS* are issued to members of the Boulder Barter Network who pay a $22 annual fee for membership, which includes a subscription to the *Boulder Barter Directory*, in which members advertise their offers and requests. Besides the annual membership fee, members pay $2 for each ad listed in the Directory. Copies of the Directory are also distributed throughout the Boulder area as a pull-out section in a local classified advertising paper called *Freeadz*.

Figure 10.6: A *Boulder HOUR* 1 Hour Note -- Face Side

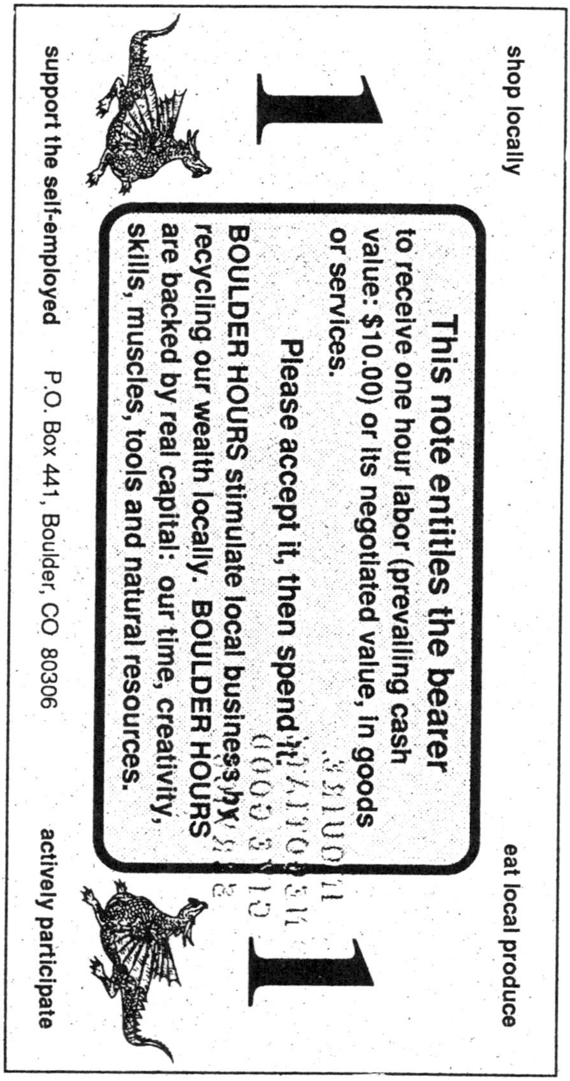

Figure 10.7: A *Boulder HOUR* 1 Hour Note -- Reverse Side

Upon joining, each member receives an amount of *HOUR* notes equal to 4 hours, which s/he is then encouraged to spend into circulation. S/he agrees, in return, to accept at least some "barter money" when s/he makes a sale. As of December 1993, there were about 125 members and the Directory contained 491 listings. *Boulder HOURS* have been issued in denominations of 1/2, 1, and 2 hours, and like its Ithaca counterpart, each *Boulder HOUR* is considered to be equivalent to about $10 of official currency. Figures 10.6 and 10.7 show the front and back sides of a 1 hour note.

Service Credits and Time Dollars

Another interesting development in cashless exchange is the service credit plan originated by Edgar Cahn. Cahn, a prominent lawyer, conceived the plan as a way of addressing the inadequacy of government programs intended to deal with social problems. He set out to create "a new kind of money," independent of government and central banks, which could be created by people themselves in the process of helping one another.

The basic idea is that a person can get credit for helping someone else now, and use those credits later to get similar services for him/herself or a family member. The plan was started with the exchange of a narrow range of services, primarily care of the elderly, education, and child care, but Cahn hopes that eventually, the range of services covered can be widely expanded.

The unit of credit in Cahn's service credit scheme is the "time dollar," equivalent to one hour of service. The intention is to exchange services on the basis of an hour for an hour. For example, when Mr. Green spends two hours of his time to help the elderly Mrs. Brown do her grocery shopping, he receives 2 time dollars credit to his account. Later, when Mr. Green is himself in need of help, he can claim 2 hours of service from someone else in the system.

Cahn, presumably because of his prominence and main-stream political contacts, has been able to gain a great deal of official support at both the state and federal levels. He states:

> "(I) got it enacted into law, first in two states and the District of Columbia. I got the IRS to rule that it was tax-exempt and not barter in the conventional sense -- in the commercial sense."[80]

The IRS ruling that service credits are tax-exempt is a major milestone and has probably been a major factor in the rapid proliferation of Time Dollar programs around the country.

As of April 1993, there were 85 operational service credit programs operating in 26 states, plus an additional 20 programs being planned. The state of Missouri alone has 37 service credit programs.[81] The Missouri state government has been so enthusiastic about the plan, that it has guaranteed the value of service credits. It will go into the market to buy services for those who have earned credits, if there is no one willing to provide services for Time Dollars when needed. In Miami, participants are earning more than 10,000 Time Dollars a month by helping others.[82]

Time dollars provide recognition for services that would ordinarily be done by volunteers. One of the main advantages is that it allows participants, *e.g.* the elderly, teenagers, the unemployed, to "redefine themselves as producers and contributors rather than recipients of charity."[83]

Cahn also cites some other important outcomes of a service credit system; the social, community-building aspect. As he puts it:

---

[80] "A Public Service Economy: An Interview with Edgar S. Cahn", *Multinational Monitor*, April 1989, pp. 17-21.

[81] *Directory of Volunteer Service Credit Programs*, University of Maryland, Center on Aging, College Park, MD, April 1993.

[82] Cahn, Edgar S., "Time Dollars", *Co-op America Quarterly*, Spring 1993.

[83] *ibid.*

"...the very process of earning credits knits groups together... They begin having pot-luck lunches; and they begin forming neighborhood crime watch things, and they begin looking after each other and checking in; and they begin to set up food bank coops. (It) seems to act as a catalyst for the creation of group cohesion in a society where that kind of catalyst is difficult to find..."[84]

---

[84] Cahn, *Multinational Monitor*, *op.cit.*

PART III COMMUNITY EMPOWERMENT AND MONETARY TRANSFORMATION

CHAPTER 11 BASIC FACTORS IN THE CREATION OF DEMOCRATIC EXCHANGE MEDIA

"Every piece of money is essentially a credit instrument."
-- Hugo Bilgram and L. E. Levy

Bilgram and Levy remind us that "every piece of money is essentially a credit instrument, an acknowledgement of debt, accepted in the market as a medium of exchange, and that its value depends solely on the value of the credit on which it is based."[85] This may not be true of full valued commodity monies like gold and silver coins, but it is certainly true of the common types of paper and "checkbook" money we have become accustomed to using in this modern era. Likewise, the contemporary local exchange examples described in the previous chapter and the democratic exchange media which we advocate and describe herein are also credit instruments.

Keeping that fact in mind, it becomes clear that the first requisite in evaluating any exchange system is to assess "the value of the credit upon which it (the money) is based." Monetary theory speaks of several essential factors which must be appropriately dealt with in order to have a sound monetary system. The most essential of these factors can be highlighted in the following questions:

1. What should be the basis upon which money is issued into circulation?
2. What factors should be used to determine the amount of money to be issued?
3. Who should have the power to issue money?
4. How should the power to issue be allocated among those empowered to issue, and what should be the limits?

---

[85] Bilgram and Levy, *op.cit.*, p. 383.

As we shall see, the answer to the second question follows naturally from the first, while the answer to the fourth question is implied by the criteria selected in answering the third.

Basis of Issue

The most important factor in the creation of an exchange medium is the **BASIS OF ISSUE**. It is my strong belief that **the creation and issuance into circulation of a unit of currency or credit should be coincident with the transfer of value**. It should also give rise to a "commitment" on the part of the original issuer to redeem the currency, in the market, by providing equivalent value in exchange for the currency, *i.e.* the issuer should be obligated to accept his currency at par or face value from those wishing to buy his/her goods or services. The form of the redemption need not necessarily be limited to a particular commodity, but may be in the form of any desired goods or services. This is the way a mutual credit system operates. The "credits" which the seller receives are, in effect, money, created by the buyer who is "committed" to redeem credits later by providing goods or services to someone in the system.[86]

Regulation of the Amount of Exchange Media Supplied

It is crucial that the quantity of the exchange medium be **balanced** with the flow of goods and services coming into the market, and that it be **self-adjusting**. Much is made of the "quantity (or volume) theory of the value of money," and it is generally accepted as valid. But as we have already shown, it is not the quantity of money per se which determines

---

[86] The use of the term "credit" may cause some confusion since it has more than one meaning. It can be said that goods are delivered on "credit". In this case the seller is giving the buyer "economic credit", i.e. trusting the buyer to pay equivalent value later. In an mutual exchange system, it is the seller's account which receives "accounting credit" on the books of the exchange, indicating that the seller has so much value "coming to him." Thus, the buyer receives economic credit (in the form of goods or services), while the seller receives the corresponding accounting credit which represents his claim to value within the system.

its value, so it is not the quantity which needs to be controlled.[87] If money is properly issued, there will never be any problem of under-supply or over-supply. The quantity of money will always be just the right amount to purchase the goods and services which it represents. Capital goods, land, purchases by consumers, and ever-expanding government debt should therefore all be excluded as allowable bases of issue. It is only the politicization of money and the monopolization of its issuance and control which have caused the focus of attention to be shifted away from its true value foundation onto its mere volume. **The proper basis of issue is the transfer of value, as it is being exchanged, from a producer to another (potential) producer.**

In a mutual credit system, credits are created as needed to mediate an exchange, and there is no interest burden on debits. The total amount of credits is always balanced with an equal amount of total debits, so there can never be an artificial shortage or surplus as there is in the official monetary system.

Power to Issue

The third important factor is the **POWER TO ISSUE**. In a truly free society, power of all kinds, including economic power, should be widely dispersed. Thus, the association of issuers should be open to anyone willing and able to abide by its agreements and rules, which should be minimal, and there should be no restriction on the formation of competing associations. Just as we have competing credit card companies, the issuance of exchange media should be open to competing associations of issuing groups. This will tend to insure that proper procedures are followed, and contribute to the innovative development of the exchange process.

So, **everyone should be empowered to issue exchange media based upon the their ability and willingness to contribute valuable goods and services to the community**. This means that an issuer should, in

---

[87] For a thorough and relatively rigorous exposition of the fallacy of the volume theory of the value of money, see Bilgram and Levy, op cit., pp. 136-155.

the normal course of business, be able to liquidate his/her issue within a reasonable period of time. The guiding principle which seems most appropriate, based on past monetary experience, is that <u>a participant is qualified to put into circulation an amount of "money" up to the amount of his/her sales over a 2 or 3 month period</u>.

Some Theoretical Considerations for Contemporary Systems

As we have seen, the soundness of currency in circulation derives from the basis upon which it is issued, and the ultimate "backing" for it is the commitment of the issuers to redeem it by the sale of goods and services.

Authority

There has been considerable debate about whether or not an issuing authority is needed for a local currency or mutual exchange system, and, if so, what the power of that authority should be. As we have pointed out, the basis of any exchange system is the agreement, either formal or tacit, among the participants. **It is the agreement that constitutes the authority under which the system operates; not the administrator or board of directors**, which, if they exist at all, are empowered only to make certain specified decisions or take limited actions, **as stated in the agreement**.

Those agreements, of whatever type, which seem to be most workable, are those which define clearly and precisely the rights and responsibilities of each of the parties to the agreement. In the case of a mutual credit system, someone has to sign-up new participants, keep the membership list, record transactions, and keep track of account balances. These functions must all be included in the agreement. Each participant is given the right to issue credits, and each participant has the obligation of redeeming the credits which s/he issues.

It is important that the participant feel this commitment strongly. This works more easily in a system in which there is formal "membership" and a **written** agreement. This agreement might require members to "settle" their accounts if and when they terminate their membership.

Thus, in a mutual credit system, a member with a debit balance would be obligated to earn enough credits to bring his/her balance to zero, or, perhaps, pay an equivalent amount in cash. Similarly, if currency notes are used, a member to whom notes have been transferred would agree to return a like amount of notes, or cash.

A periodic renewal of membership provides an opportunity for each member to confirm his/her commitment. If a person fails to renew his/her membership, then the management could "call" his/her commitment. The obvious question though is, how shall the agreement be enforced? I believe that a community-based exchange system, in contrast to the dominant system with which we are all familiar, should not depend upon legal enforcement of contracts. As with any voluntary association, there should be no penalties for failure to honor one's commitment, except for that of expulsion from the association. In a limited, local, more personal system, we can probably do without a formal enforcement mechanism of coercion and penalties, trusting instead the good faith of the members, and the subtle social pressures which regulate behavior in any community.

Though neither the nominal LETS system nor *Ithaca HOURS* strictly follow all the theoretical direction suggested above, they seem to be working well. This is probably due to the intensive educational efforts mounted by their proponents and the strong community spirit in the areas where they have prospered. In the case of *Ithaca HOURS*, it is probably also due to the rapid growth in the number of participants and close control over the amount of *HOURS* placed in circulation. With only about 5 to 6 *HOURS* per participant issued, there should be little risk of *HOURS* being discounted in the market. As the system grows, however, the need for more formal protocols will likely become apparent.

The Unit of Account

Since the Ithaca notes are denominated in "HOURS" rather than dollars, they seem to have acquired a market value which is somewhat independent of that of the ever-declining value of Federal Reserve currency. Even though the "HOUR," as a distinctive unit of account, is not precisely defined, it is still possible for people to make a mental distinction between "hours" and "dollars." It appears that people have largely accepted Glover's assessment of the *HOUR* as being worth about $10. This amount might be considered to be some kind of local average wage. If the further debasement of the dollar should cause wages to rise significantly, say to $14 on the average, the *HOUR* notes might then pass for goods or services worth $14 instead of $10, provided, of course, that *HOUR* notes have been properly issued and not themselves debased.

In a LETS system, the unit of account is the "green dollar," or whatever the local group wishes to call it (*e.g. cowries, credits, oaks* etc.). People naturally equate the value of a "green dollar" to that of an official dollar since, unlike the Ithaca situation, they have no other referent. Green dollars would undoubtedly depreciate along with the official dollar as inflation proceeds. This is one more reason to circulate them rapidly and avoid holding them as a savings medium.

Eventually, local currency and exchange systems will need to define a different unit of account. I would prefer something more precise than labor time, like the unit of account based on a composite commodity standard, as I proposed in my book, *Money and Debt: A Solution to the Global Crisis*[88]. Such a standard, based on a "market basket" of commodities, would tend to be both stable and apolitical.

Alternatively, some single commodity which has special importance for the local economy could be used as a standard of value for a local currency. This could be a cord of wood, a bushel of corn, a bale of cotton, or some other commodity which is widely traded in local commerce. However, a unit of account based on a single commodity has certain drawbacks. Its value is more influenced by transitory conditions like weather, and the market for a single commodity can be more easily manipulated by governments and large volume traders.

---

[88] Greco, *op.cit.*, Section III.

What About Backing and Redeemability?

Many present day monetary reformers lament the passing of the redemption feature of paper currency and bank credit. They yearn for a return to the "gold standard," by which they mean, not only the definition of the dollar in terms of a particular weight of gold, but also the redeemability of paper currency into gold. In the past, paper money was redeemable, at the option of the holder, for silver or gold coins. This option of exchanging one kind of money for another did indeed play a major role in keeping political paper money honest by limiting the amount of paper which could be issued. The reinstitution of redeemability would certainly be one way of restoring discipline upon the issuing authorities, but it would have negative side-effects and is far from the ideal approach.

The desire for redeemability in a currency is an anachronistic bit of psychology left over from the days when money had substance. Paper bills and bank credit began as "claim checks" against specie, or real money, *i.e.* gold and silver. Thus, there were actually two kinds of money, paper and specie (gold or silver). The "real" money was, of course, the metal, and the paper was only a symbolic representation of it.

Under such a system redeemability was absolutely necessary to prevent the banks and/or other issuing authorities from issuing too much paper. With expanding economic activity, however, there was a chronic shortage of metallic money. This led to the expedient of what is known as "fractional reserve banking," in which banks were allowed to issue paper money in amounts that were several times the value of their gold holdings. The paper was still redeemable for gold but there was not enough gold to redeem all the paper. The potential problem with such a system is obvious, and indeed, bank runs and panics were recurrent and common. The issuance of paper was often unsound (and, therefore, excessive), and whenever the public got a sense of this they exercised their option to redeem paper for gold, depleting bank reserves.

Unfortunately, rather than ending the abuses and developing a sound system, the monetary authorities addressed the problem of bank runs by centralizing control of the banking system and putting an end to redeemability. Thus they eliminated the only effective means of imposing discipline upon the issuers and opened the way for abuse on a grand scale. Discipline is certainly necessary in a monetary system, especially when the issuer has a monopoly and competing currencies may be excluded from the marketplace. In a free environment, however, there are better ways to impose discipline. The ultimate test of a currency is its acceptability in the marketplace and its "redeemability" for goods and services there. When traders have the freedom to refuse to accept a currency, or to accept it at a discount from its face value, then they can protect themselves from the effects of improper and excessive issuance of a currency. In the words of Friedrich von Hayek:

> "There could be no more effective check against the abuse of money by government [*or any other issuer*] than if people were free to refuse any money they distrusted and to prefer money in which they had confidence."[89]

In any event, computers and communications technologies have long since obviated the need for "claim check" kinds of money. Rather than revert to this anachronistic form of discipline, it is now necessary to move away from monopolized, political, and coercive monetary systems toward free, non-governmental, democratic exchange media.

What then will provide the "backing" for a democratic, privately issued, credit type of money which we are considering? This question was answered very well by E. C. Riegel:

> " 'Reserves' and metal hoards are but window dressing. Only that which is purchasable is back of money. (p.109).

> "...like any money unit, until something has been exchanged for it, nothing is back of it. When it has been exchanged for something, that something is back of it. Money's material backing is that which the

---

[89] Hayek, Friedrich von, *Choice in Currency: A Way to Stop Inflation*. London: Institute of Economic Affairs, 1976.

seller surrenders in exchange for it; its moral backing is the buyer's promise to back it with an equivalent value when in turn he becomes the seller."[90]

Implementation

Whether it involves a mutual credit system, a circulating paper currency, or both, any alternative exchange system, in order to be easily implemented and readily accepted, should, as much as possible, use familiar devices and procedures. People are accustomed to using paper notes (bills), checks, bank accounts, debit cards and credit cards, and these inventions have demonstrated their effectiveness in handling the processes of trade. These are the mechanical aspects of money and banking and there is no reason why the new, democratic, local exchange systems should not use similar devices.

It might be wise, however, for local exchange systems to use different terminology and completely avoid the use of words like "money," and "dollar" to preclude confusion with, and any suggestion of competition with existing monetary and financial structures. Local exchange media are complementary to official media and might be referred to as "coupons," "credits," or "scrip." They will develop in parallel with official monetary systems, and, over time, assume a larger and larger portion of the burden of mediating exchange. As people gain experience with them, they will come to understand the simple essence of exchange media, and sense the economic empowerment which community control provides.

---

[90] Riegel, *Private Enterprise Money*, *op.cit.*

CHAPTER 12 COMMUNITY EMPOWERMENT THROUGH MUTUAL CREDIT SYSTEMS

"There was probably no other person in the whole country who had meditated so much on the question of interest. Maragaya's mind was full of it. Night and day he sat and brooded over it. The more he thought of it the more it seemed to him the greatest wonder of creation. It combined in it the mystery of birth and multiplication. Otherwise how could you account for the fact that a hundred rupees in a savings bank became one hundred and twenty in course of time? It was something like the ripening corn. Every rupee, Maragaya felt, contained in it the seed of another rupee, and that seed in it another seed and so on and on to infinity. It was something like the firmament, endless stars and within each star an endless firmament and within each an further endless... It bordered on mystic perception. It gave him the feeling of being part of an infinite existence.

R. K. Narayan, *The Financial Expert*.

An exchange system may utilize any of a number of instruments and protocols. It may utilize physical objects which circulate from hand-to-hand, such as paper notes, coins or tokens; it may be comprised of accounts and ledgers using debits and credits; or it may involve some combination of these. Whatever form the exchange media may take, whether paper notes or account balances, the same basic principles apply. In general, from this point on, when we speak of "currency," it should be understood that the term also includes credits in a ledger (bookkeeping) system.

What is Mutual Credit (MC)?

Anyone familiar with the LETS system already has a basic understanding of what mutual credit (MC) looks like. Mutual credit is the generic term which includes ledger systems like LETS but isn't limited to the particular procedures and protocols which LETS uses. It might, like LETS, use a ledger or system of accounts for recording the initial obligations of its members, while also providing its members with circulating notes. These notes would be issued to members against their credit lines, in effect, providing a physical representation of that credit. Just as a cash withdrawal is debited against (subtracted from) a bank account, the amount of any notes thus issued would be debited against the member's Mutual Credit account.

A mutual credit (MC) system is designed to surmount the limitations of barter. Like money, it provides an intermediary device which allows two parties to trade even though one of them may have nothing the other wants. For example, suppose Martha knits sweaters, and John wants to buy one but has nothing that Martha presently needs. Using mutual credit (MC), he can still get the sweater, giving Martha "credits" for the agreed price. Where does John get the credits to give to Martha? He creates them. Just as banks create dollars to give to someone who requests a loan, John creates the credits to pay Martha for the sweater. Martha can then spend her credits when she buys something from anyone else in the system. When John creates credits to pay Martha, he obligates himself to accept credits from someone in the system at some future time in payment for his own goods or services. In this way, by making a sale, he "redeems" the credits which he originally issued. This is shown pictorially in Figure 12.1. It can be seen that the process is essentially identical to that of the ideal money circuit which we described in Chapter 2, and the LETS trading circuit described in Chapter 10.

In a mutual credit system, the people empower themselves to do the same thing that banks have done for years, essentially creating their own money in the form of credit, but saving the cost of interest, while distributing the money themselves according to their own needs. In such a system, holding credits is evidence that so much value has been delivered to the community, while a debit balance represents that person's commitment to deliver value to the community sometime in the near future.

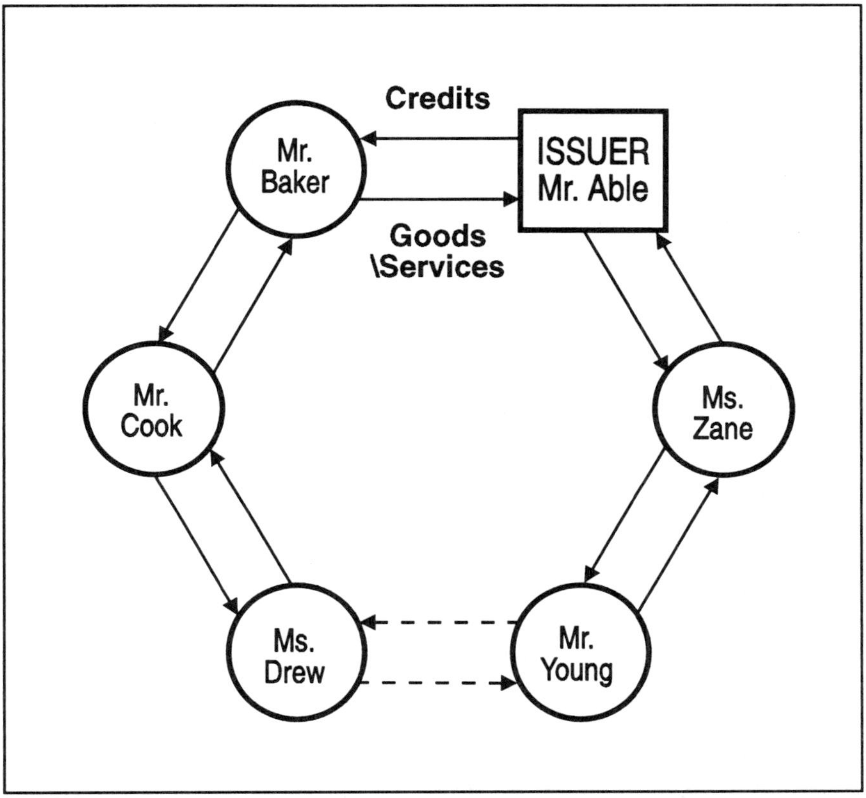

Figure 12.1: The Mutual Credit Trading Cycle

How a Mutual Credit System Works

Mutual Credit can be viewed as an extension of the long-established practice of trade credit which businesses offer to one another in the normal course of business. They simply sell to their customers on what is called "open account," which means that they deliver the merchandise and bill their customer for the amount due. A certain amount of time is allowed for payment to be made. It may be 15, 30, or 60 days, or more, depending on the customs of that particular line of business. Often, a discount may be given for prompt payment. In the terminology of business, an example of typical trade terms might be "2%/10; net 30 days," which means that payment is due within 30 days of the billing date, but a 2% discount may be taken if payment is made within 10 days.

The basic idea of a Mutual Credit system is to extend the practice of trade credit to a wider group of participants, each of whom has the power to buy without cash, and, at the same time, to lengthen the duration within which balances may be outstanding. The ideal, at least with respect to empowerment of the participants and local control of the local economy, is to eliminate completely the requirement of payment in official currency.

Over the long-run individual account balances will move up and down, some months ending with a credit balance and some months ending with a debit balance, but averaging out around a balance of zero. As long as debit balances do not become chronic or extreme, the system can handle these situations readily; indeed, since the total of credits must be balanced by an equal amount of total debits, outstanding debit balances are a necessary feature of the system and will have no adverse effect upon its operation. If a particular participant develops a chronic debit balance, steps can be taken by the group to help him/her to increase sales and/or reduce purchases. This issue will be considered in more detail later on.

Basic Steps in Organizing a Mutual Credit System

The following are the essential steps in starting a Mutual Credit trading system:

1. Organize a core group of people to begin trading among themselves using trade credit units as the exchange medium. It is best if the founding group is composed of people who know one another or who have been working together for some time. The group can be expanded, as appropriate, by inviting other friends and acquaintances to join. New members might be provisional for some specified period of time, after which they would have the same status as founding members. Provisional members might have a debit limit which is lower than the limit for full members.

2. Choose some unique name for the system credits to distinguish them from official currency. They might be called "sand dollars," "green dollars," "LETS credits," "creds," etc. To help avoid confusion, it might be best to avoid using the word "dollar" in naming the local unit.

3. Establish some means for members to make known to one another their needs and offerings. This can be easily done by distributing a newsletter containing classified ads listing both offers of and requests for items and services.

4. Limit the debit balances on member accounts. Initially, every full member account should have the same maximum debit balance. The amount is a matter for debate but an equivalent of about $200 or $300 might be reasonable to start with. As trading develops, debit limits might be raised for those who demonstrate the capacity to carry a higher amount by selling more within the system.

5. Designate someone to be "registrar" for the system to maintain the membership list and record members' transactions. Members will report their transactions using a standard form. The registrar will periodically update members' account balances and issue account statements.

6. Produce and distribute periodically to all members a summary report showing each member's balance and trading volume for the previous period. This will help to establish a completely open information system and allow every member to know the health of the system and be aware of any developing problems.

7. Designate someone to produce a newsletter and/or an updated list of requests and offerings. This could be part of the registrar's duties, or it could be done by someone else.

8. Charge a certain amount for each service provided by the system. There should be fixed charges for recording transactions, advertising offers and requests, generating and mailing account statements and reports, and, perhaps, providing a membership directory. Some of

these fees will be in system credits, but some will need to be charged in cash to cover cash expenses for postage, copy expenses, or supplies which may not available within the system. These revenues to the system might also be supplemented by charging an annual membership fee.

9. Charge a small percentage, in system credits, at the end of each period on all balances, both credit and debit. The percentage charged should be the same for both types of balance. This will have several positive effects. It is intended mainly to stimulate the circulation of credits and avoid stagnation of balances. In addition, it will provide a supplementary source of system credits with which to pay for system operation and development. This will assure more adequate compensation for the registrar, newsletter editor, and others who provide services to the system. Any surpluses which develop might be used to fund community projects or for other purposes which the members shall determine by consensus.

10. Schedule regular gatherings of the membership. These are not just to take care of system business, but to get to know one another, to trade, and to have some fun. Try pot-luck suppers, picnics, auctions, and rummage sales.

As the MC system develops, members will likely find that they are supporting one another in a variety of ways -- as friends, confidants, counselors, etc.. Some direct barter and informal trading will occur. This should be encouraged rather than discouraged. Even though private and informal transactions by-pass the system and avoid paying fees into it, they also reduce the work load. The primary objective, after all, is to foster the development of mutually supportive relationships. If the system works for people, they will help to maintain it through donations and volunteer labor. Sometimes, it's better not to keep score.

Continuing Issues in Mutual Credit Systems

The above steps and suggestions are based on limited experience and are by no means the final word on the matter. Each group will have to work out for itself many of the answers to the recurrent problems of exchange.

The questions and issues that need to be addressed in establishing and operating a mutual credit system are essentially the same as those which exist in any system of money and banking, and if not properly handled can lead to disastrous consequences. Various groups have dealt with them in different ways, but some approaches are superior to others. These issues are summarized as follows:

Debit limits.
How are limits on individual accounts to be set? What amounts are reasonable in allowing members maximum purchasing power without becoming a drag on the system? What provisions should be made for monitoring accounts and correcting imbalances?

Account settlement agreements.
How long should account balances be allowed to remain stagnant? What should be done when a member drops out? What provisions, if any, should be made for periodic clearing or settlement of accounts?

Savings and Investment Provisions.
Should account balances serve as savings and investment media? If not, how can such use be limited. What mechanisms should be provided for savings and investment, if any?

Interest/Demurrage on Account Balances.
Should interest and/or demurrage charges be levied on debit and/or credit balances?

Co-responsibility groups.
Should members be allowed to participate as individuals or should everyone be a part of an affinity group in which the group members take some responsibility for each others' balances?

Group/organizational/family memberships.
Should the system provide fee discounts to people who join as part of an organization, group, or family, and if so, how much? How is "family" defined? What limitations should be placed on family or group memberships, if any?

Taxability/Reportability.
There is a considerable amount of confusion and controversy about whether cashless trading is taxable, either constitutionally or under IRS regulations, and whether or not members need to report their trading on their tax returns. If trades are reported, should the seller report the credits s/he received or should the buyer report the value of the goods and services s/he received? Which party has received income? Is the system administrator responsible for reporting members' business to the IRS?

Advertising and Transaction fees.
How much should be charged for publishing notices/ads and recording transactions? What portion of the charges should be charged in official currency and what portion in system "credits"? How can meeting the general cash needs for operating the system be assured?

Preventing Stagnation in Mutual Credit Systems

One problem which may arise in any system of exchange, and which is worthy of special attention, is stagnation of circulation. In a mutual credit system, stagnation takes the form of idle balances, either debit or credit. Those holding debit balances have bought more than they've sold. If such an account is idle, that member, in effect, is not honoring her/his commitment to the members of the system in a timely manner. Having received value, s/he is "committed" to deliver like value. Although there may be no specified time limit for honoring such a commitment, there is the expectation that efforts will be made to move the account balance back toward zero. Some activity in earning credits shows "good faith" and indicates that a member is willing and able to provide something the community needs or wants. If a member does develop a chronic debit balance, however, it needs to be handled in some way.

In keeping with the basic principles of a local, limited, personal and convivial system, chronic debit balances should not be dealt with in a punitive fashion. A mutual credit system is designed to be friendly and helpful rather than dominating and manipulative. A chronic debit balance may be indicative that a member is having some kind of personal trouble, in which case fellow members would probably want to help in some way. Perhaps that member needs to improve the quality of the products or services s/he provides, or perhaps s/he needs to acquire some new skill to provide something the community needs. In a personal, local system, these matters can be handled in a helpful way, by those closest to the problem, rather than impersonally and coercively by distant and unresponsive bureaucracies.

Those holding credit balances in a mutual credit system, have sold more than they've bought. If an account with a credit balance is idle, that member, in effect, is not demanding from the system value which is due him/her. Having delivered value, s/he is entitled to receive like value. Although there may be no specified time limit within which credits must be spent, the expectation is that credits will be spent, not saved. Saving credits has the effect of preventing, to some extent, those with debit balances from selling enough to get back to zero.

The primary problem to be overcome in facilitating trade is the "barter limitation," *i.e.* the fact that the buyer may not have anything the seller wants. By creating an intermediary "medium of exchange," *e.g.* trade credits, there is a "space" created within which the seller may supply the buyer's need anyway, and then proceed to find a supplier for his/her own need. This "space" is only partially temporal; mostly it is interpersonal, a matter of matching up specific needs or wants with appropriate supplies in the market. In other words, it allows some slack in which people can find one another so that each can have his/her needs satisfied.

Saving and Investment

Another necessary function in finance is the storage of value. When economists speak of money as being also a "store of value," they are speaking metaphorically. Since value is an abstract concept and not a physical quantity, it cannot really be stored. Cabbages can be stored, wheat can be stored, building materials can be stored, metals can be stored, but each, of course, is subject to some degree of spoilage or deterioration over time. The primary problem to be solved by storage is the asynchronicity of supply and demand.

The very idea of storage is based on the desire to match present supplies with future needs. We put aside the extra food from the garden in summer to satisfy our hunger next winter when the garden will not be producing. Similarly, we save during our productive years so that we can have the means of livelihood during our retirement years. But unlike our storage of food from the garden, which we do directly, our saving for retirement we do socially. Saving, in financial terms, must involve other people.

Ultimately, at any point in time, non-producers, such as young children and retirees, are dependent upon then current producers for the satisfaction of their material needs and desires. The mechanisms by which non-producer needs are met are varied and often complex and are based on such factors as cultural values, ethics, social norms, legal statutes and financial agreements. In our retirement years for example, we are mainly dependent upon two basic arrangements: (1) legislated, involuntary redistribution of wealth by governments in the form of such programs as FICA taxes (Social Security) and Welfare and, (2) contractual agreements of a form usually called "investments" which consist of such financial instruments as pensions, insurance, annuities, stocks, bonds, mutual fund shares, bank deposits, etc..

Both legislated programs and investments provide the recipient with a "claim" against current and/or future production. The question as to which claims may or may not be "legitimate" is, of course, always open to debate and disagreement, and the questions of which claims may or may not be honored is always a matter of concern. The satisfaction of any claim is always dependent upon the ability and willingness of those who are asked to bear its burden.

What About Interest?

Given our cultural conditioning and the prevailing practice within the conventional systems of money and finance, there is a tendency to want to impose a levy or charge upon debit balances, these balances being thought of as loans to the "debitor," and the levy representing an interest charge. Considering what has been said above, it should be clear that such attitudes and practices need to be reconsidered.

In accordance with the rationale put forth by Silvio Gesell, some have argued that, in order to keep an exchange system vital, a periodic levy should be made upon credit (positive) balances. This kind of charge is known as "demurrage."[91] The argument is that demurrage would encourage the spending and discourage the holding, or saving, of currency or credit balances, and insure the lively flow of "money" (credits) through the system. That is not to say that saving is "bad," but that it should be accomplished using some medium other than the exchange medium.[92]

The imposition of levies upon either debit or credit balances, or both, will undoubtedly promote their use as an exchange medium, deter their use as a savings/investment medium, and prevent stagnation. However, such levies may have a negative effect upon another primary objective, that of "reciprocity." The idea of reciprocity is that the value received by a trader should be equivalent to the value which he/she delivered. The discriminatory imposition of a levy upon only one or the other type of balance upsets this ideal. The case for imposing levies upon balances is a strong one. However, since everyone benefits from the operation of the system, if a levy is imposed upon balances, both debit balances and credit balances should be charged equally.

Current Account *vs.* Capital Account

Another possible approach to dealing with the problem of idle balances would be to limit both the amount of debit and credit which could be carried over from one period to the next. Any amount in excess of the limit would be "cleared" to a capital account. Anyone who cannot clear his/her debit at the end of the current period, or who wants long-term financing for any purpose, would have to find someone willing to assign his/her credits for a specified period of time. This is a capital market function. Likewise, anyone who desires to "save" his/her credits, must

[91] The cost of the stamp used in stamp scrip is a form of demurrage.

[92] For a more complete elaboration on this point, see Greco, *op.cit.*, pp 54-59.

find some suitable investment medium for accomplishing the storage of his/her value. In other words, side-by-side with the exchange system, there would exist a capital market which would provide for capital formation (investment) and savings (storage of value).

As an example, suppose that at the end of the quarter, Betty has a credit balance of 900, but the maximum that may be carried over is 500. She must then find someone who needs the remaining 400 credits and make a private deal with him/her, or she might "deposit" her excess credits in a savings coop which would invest them for her.

Suppose too that Gary wants to acquire enough credits to hire George to help him build a house. They agree on a price of 2,000 credits. But since the debit limit on all current accounts is, say, 500, Gary must "borrow" the remaining 1,500. He could make a deal with Betty, and maybe two or three other members, to use their excess credits for some specified period of time. During that time, of course, Betty would not be able to use those credits herself. Alternatively, Gary could go to the savings cooperative and request a loan of 1,500 credits.

Capital formation is the process of creating the means of production, including the creation of new businesses or the expansion and improvement of existing ones. It includes construction of buildings, improvement of land, production of tools and equipment, and other expenditures which are expected to be recovered over a long period of time through the sale of products or services. The creation of exchange media should be based upon the exchange of current supplies of goods and services. It is a well-established principle of sound banking that long-term assets should not be used as the basis for creating new money, but should be financed out of "savings," *i.e.* money which has already been created but not spent on current consumption.

Having both a "current" account and a "capital" account is a way of separating the "medium of exchange" from the "store of value." It is as easy as transferring deposits from your checking account to your savings account, or writing a check to buy shares of stock or a mutual fund. Indeed, along with empowering people by allowing them to create their own exchange medium, it is still important to follow sound banking practices. Since these practices have been largely forgotten and abandoned by the established monetary and financial institutions, new systems must be built from the ground up. These systems should be based upon the principles of equity (just), conviviality (open to all) and reciprocity (mutual/cooperative), and a clear understanding of the effects of various financial practices.

In either case, whether in a current account or a capital account, a credit balance represents a "claim," and the activity which gives rise to the claim should determine whether it is "current" or "capital." In the current account, a credit is a short-term claim upon the market, which is intended only to facilitate trade. It is a "demand" deposit which the market should be able to satisfy at any time. In the capital account, a credit is a claim against long-lived assets which are not liquid, but will produce benefits over a long period of time. For example, if the claim has resulted from activity which has produced a building or equipment, it will take time for the cost of these to be recovered. This recovery takes place in the normal course of their use in the production and sale of consumable goods.

One of the "sins" of the present banking establishment is that it has blurred this distinction between savings deposits (time deposits) and demand (checking account) deposits, and has issued money on the basis of, not only goods on the way to market, but also goods being taken from the market.[93] Properly, demand deposits represent goods (and services) presently in the market, available for purchase, and savings deposits represent investments in capital goods and durables. Formerly, banks paid no interest on demand deposits because such deposits had to be kept available for payment of checks drawn upon the account. Thus, they could not be invested in longer-term, interest-earning assets. Now, banks are paying interest on demand deposits and giving some savings deposits much the same liquidity as demand deposits.

---

[93] For a more complete explanation of this banking error, see Appendix B, which contains excerpts from "The Lost Art of Commercial Banking" by E. C. Harwood, in *How Safe Is Your Bank*, published by the American Institute for Economic Research, Great Barrington, MA 01230, 1989.

A STORY OF ROBINSON CRUSOE: An Introduction to the Theory of Interest by Silvio Gesell[94]

Robinson Crusoe, as is well known, built his house, from motives of health, on the south side of the mountain, whereas his crops grew on the damp but fruitful northern slopes. He was therefore obliged to carry his harvests over the mountain. To eliminate this labor he decided to construct a canal around the mountain. The time required for this enterprise, to avoid silting, would have to be carried out without interruption, he estimated at three years.

He slaughtered some pigs, and cured their flesh with salt; he filled a deep trench with wheat, covering it carefully with earth. He tanned a dozen buckskins for suits and nailed them up in a chest, enclosing also the stink-glands of a skunk as a precaution against moths. In short, he provided amply, and as he thought, wisely, for the coming three years.

As he sat calculating for the last time whether his "capital" was sufficient for the projected undertaking, he was startled by the approach of a stranger, obviously the survivor of a shipwreck.

"Hallo, Crusoe!" shouted the stranger as he approached, "my ship has gone down, but I like your island and intend to settle here. Will you help me with some provisions until I have brought a field into cultivation and harvested my first crops?"

At these words, Crusoe's thoughts flew from his provisions to the possibility of interest and the attractions of life as a gentleman of independent means. He hastened to answer "yes."

"That's splendid!" replied the stranger, "but I must say at once that I shall pay no interest. I would prefer to keep myself alive by hunting

[94] Edited and adapted from Silvio Gesell, *The Natural Economic Order*.

and fishing, for my religion forbids me to pay, or to receive, interest."

Robinson Crusoe: An admirable religion! But from what motive do you expect me to advance you provisions from my stores if you pay me no interest?
Stranger: From pure egoism, my dear fellow, from your self-interest rightly understood. Because you gain, and gain enormously.

R.C.: That, stranger, you have yet to prove. I confess that I can see no advantage in lending you my provisions free of interest.
S.: I shall prove it in black and white, and if you can follow my proof, you will agree to loan without interest, and thank me into the bargain. I need, first of all, clothes, for, as you see, I am naked. Have you a supply of clothes?

R.C.: That chest is packed with buckskin suits.
S.: My dear Crusoe! I had more respect for your intelligence. Just fancy nailing up clothes for three years in a chest -- buckskins, the favorite diet of moths! And buckskins must be kept aired and rubbed with grease, otherwise they become hard and brittle.

R.C.: That is true, but I have no choice in the matter. They would be no safer in my clothes cupboard -- less safe, indeed, for it is infested by rats and mice as well as by moths.
S.: The mice will get them in any case. Look how they have already started to gnaw their way in!

R.C.: Confound the brutes! I am helpless against them.
S.: What! A human being helpless against mice! I will show you how to protect yourself against rats and mice and moths, against thieves and brittleness, dust and mildew. Lend me those clothes for one, two or three years, and I will agree to make you new clothes as soon as you require them. You will receive as many suits as you have lent me, and the new suits will be far superior to those you would have taken from this chest. Nor will you regret the absence of the particular perfume you have employed! Do you agree?

R.C.: Yes, stranger, I agree to lend you the chest of clothes; I see that in this case, the loan, even without interest, is to my advantage.
S.: Now show me your wheat; I need some for bread and seed.

R.C.: It is buried in this mound.
S.: Wheat buried for three years! What about mildew and beetles?

R.C.: I have thought about them and considered every other possibility, but this is the best I can do.
S.: Just bend down a moment. Observe the beetle crawling on the surface of the mound. Note the garbage and the spreading patch of mildew. It is high time to take out and air the wheat.

R.C.: This capital will be my ruin! If I only could find some method of protecting myself against the thousand destructive forces of nature!
S.: Let me tell you, Crusoe, how we manage at home. We build a dry and airy shed and shake out the wheat on a boarded floor. Every three weeks the whole mass is turned over with wooden shovels. We also keep a number of cats; we set mouse traps and insure against fire. In this way we keep the annual depreciation down to ten percent.

R.C.: But the labor and expense!
S.: Exactly! You shrink from the labor and expense. In that case you have another course. Lend me your wheat and I shall replace it pound for pound, sack for sack, with fresh wheat from my harvest. You thus save the labor of building a shed and turning over the wheat; you need feed no cats, you avoid the loss of weight, and instead of mouldy rubbish, you will have fresh nutritious wheat.

R.C.: With all my heart, I accept your proposal.
S.: That is you will lend me your wheat free of interest?

R.C.: Certainly; without interest and with my best thanks.
S.: But I can only use part of the wheat, I do not need it all.

R.C.: Suppose I give you the whole store with the understanding that for every ten sacks lent you give me back nine sacks?

S.: I must decline your offer, for it would mean interest - not indeed positive, but negative interest. The receiver, not the giver of the loan would be a capitalist, and my religion does not permit usury; even negative interest is forbidden. I propose therefore the following agreement. Entrust me with the supervision of your wheat, the construction of the shed, and whatever else is necessary. In return, you can pay me, annually, from every ten sacks two sacks as wages.

R.C.: It makes no difference to me whether your service comes under the heading of usury or labor. The agreement is, then, that I give you ten sacks and you give me back eight sacks?
S.: But I need other articles, a plough, a cart and tools. Do you consent to lend them, also, without interest? I promise to return everything in perfect order, a new spade for a new spade, a new, unrusted, chain for a new chain, and so forth.

R.C.: Of course I consent. All I have at present from my stores is work. Lately the river overflowed and flooded the shed, covering everything with mud. Then a storm blew off the roof and everything was damaged by rain. Now we have drought, and the wind is blowing in sand and dust. Rust, decay, breakage, drought, light, darkness, dry-rot, ants, keep up a never-ending attack. We can congratulate ourselves here upon having, at least, no thieves and incendiaries. I am delighted that, by means of a loan, I can now store my belongings without expense, labor, loss or vexation, until I need them later.
S.: That is, you now see the advantage you gain by lending me your provisions free of interest?

R.C.: Of course I do. But the question now occurs to me, why do similar stores of provisions at home bring their possessors interest?
S.: The explanation lies in money which is there the medium of such transactions.

R.C.: What? The cause of interest lies in money? That is impossible, ...
S.: .... From their nature and destination your goods are the purest form of what is usually called capital. I challenge you to take up the

position of a capitalist towards me. I need your stuff. No worker ever appeared before a capitalist as naked as I stand before you. Never has there been so clear an illustration of the relation between the owner of capital and the individual in need of capital. And now make the attempt to exact interest! Shall we begin our bargaining again from the beginning?

R.C.: I surrender! Rats, moths and rust have broken my power as a capitalist. But tell me, what is your explanation of interest?
S.: The explanation is simple enough. If there were a monetary system on this island and I, as a shipwrecked traveller, needed a loan, I would have to apply to a money-lender for money to buy the things which you have just lent me without interest. But a money-lender has not to worry about rats, moths, rust and roof-repairing, so I could not have taken up the position towards him that I have taken up towards you. The loss inseparable from the ownership of goods (there is a dog running off with one of your -- or rather my -- buckskins!) is borne, not by money-lenders, but by those who have to store the goods. The money-lender is free from such cares and is unmoved by the ingenious arguments which found the joints in your armor. You did not nail up your chest of buckskins when I refused to pay interest; the nature of your capital made you willing to continue the negotiations. Not so the money-capitalist; he would bang the door of his strong-room before my face if I announced that I would pay no interest. Yet, I do not need the money itself, I only need money to buy buckskins. The buckskins you give me without interest; but upon the money to buy buckskins I must pay interest!

R.C.: Then the cause of interest is to be sought in money? And Marx is wrong?
S.: Of course Marx is wrong. He underestimated the importance of money, the nervous system of economic life, so it is not surprising that he went wrong on other things of fundamental importance. Like all his disciples he made the mistake of excluding money from the scope of his inquiry. He was fascinated by the shining metal disks, otherwise he could never have used the following words: "Gold and silver are not by nature money, but money is by nature gold and

silver, witness the coincidence of their natural properties with its functions."

R.C.: Practice certainly does not agree with Marx's theory -- that has been clearly proved by our negotiations. Money is for Marx only a medium of exchange; but money does more, it seems, than "merely pay the price of the goods it purchases." When the borrower refuses to pay interest, the banker can bang the door of his safe without experiencing any of the cares which beset the owner of goods (capital) -- that is the root of the matter.

S.: Rats, moths and rust are powerful logicians! A single hour of economic practice has taught you more than years of study of the text-books.

CHAPTER 13 CURRENCY ALTERNATIVES FOR IMPERSONAL MARKETS

An effective community is a process, an ongoing collection of interactions and continuing relationships.
-- Michael Linton

Up to this point, our consideration of exchange alternatives, specifically, local currencies and mutual credit systems, has emphasized the importance of personal commitment within relatively small, limited communities of cooperators. The social dynamics which exist within such groups are a very important element in assuring the workability of these approaches. The social and economic interrelationships within a community are mutually reinforcing and evolve simultaneously.

The formation of mutual credit systems such as LETS is one approach to building community while mobilizing the productive potential of labor which has been undervalued by the market or marginalized by the dominant national and global systems. The building of community is not just a by-product, but an essential requirement if human needs are to be adequately satisfied. But there may be other ways "to get from here to there." There may be some places and circumstances in which a less direct approach might be more workable, at least as an intermediate step.

As Michael Linton expresses it, "Most regions are communities only in name rather than reality. **An effective community is a process, an ongoing collection of interactions and continuing relationships.**"[95] Where these ongoing interactions and continuing relationships are lacking, it might be more effective to approach the problem of exchange by implementing a currency system involving commitments which are more formal and conventional. One such approach would be a commodity-based currency.

---

[95] *Local Currencies*, brief, Landsman Community Services, May 8, 1991.

A Commodity-based Currency

In an impersonal environment, one may know little or nothing about his/her potential trading partners. In that instance it becomes expedient to have a currency which represents a claim to valuable property. Such a currency would tend toward the "hard," impersonal pole of the spectrum, but the system for issuing and regulating it could, nonetheless, be very democratic. The value of such a currency can be assured by some kind of "cover," *i.e.* it would be a "funded" currency.

Funded *vs.* Non-funded Currencies and Exchange Systems

The local currency and mutual exchange systems discussed thus far have been non-funded. Non-funded currencies are characterized as follows:

1. A non-funded currency is one which is issued on the basis of some exchange transaction or agreement. No assets are held by the issuing agency and the currency is therefore not redeemable, except, of course, in the market, for goods and services.

2. The currency may be issued on the basis of the transfer of value between two parties, one of which (the buyer) is authorized to issue such currency under an agreement with others willing to accept it in payment.[96]

3. The "backing" for a non-funded currency is simply the formal or implied commitment of the buyer to deliver equal value to someone at some future time in return for the local currency which s/he has created and issued. Thus, s/he "redeems" it by making a sale.

4. As we have already pointed out, there must be a limit to the amount of currency which each individual party to the agreement can issue. This limit should be determined by his/her ability to produce. Experience indicates that the limit should not exceed the value

---

[96] An individual may, of course, issue his own currency (his I.O.U.) by his own authority; however, its acceptability will be limited in comparison to a currency which many people are committed, by agreement, to accept.

equivalent to his/her normal sales volume within a 2 or 3 month period.

The essential features of a funded currency or credit system are as follows:

1. A funded currency is one which is issued on the basis of the transfer to the issuing agency of some valuable assets which are held as "reserves."

2. These assets are held by the issuing agency against future redemption of the currency. The currency may be redeemable on demand of the holder, or it's redemption may be restricted in some way. It may be redeemable only at certain times, or under certain specified conditions, and/or only by certain specified individuals or groups.

3. The assets which are accepted can be in most any form, however, some assets serve the purpose better than others. Historically, gold and silver have often served this purpose, along with government bonds and other securities, or even other currencies. Some "third world" countries use U.S. dollars as reserves for their national currencies.

4. It is best to use assets which represent value on the way to market or assets which can be easily liquidated in fractional amounts. Thus, the use of real estate or capital equipment is not recommended, unless the rate of redemption is restricted to conform to the productivity or rate of liquidation of such assets in the normal course of business.

5. One of the usual errors which banks and governments have made is to issue more currency notes than the value of the assets held. This is known as "fractional reserve banking."

6. To be "fully funded," the amount of currency issued must not exceed the value of the assets held for redemption.

7. If the value of the assets held should decline in terms of some other currency or value measure, the value of the currency itself would decline in relation to that same measure.

8. If some official currency, such as the U.S. Dollar, or securities denominated in dollars, are used as backing (reserves) for a funded local currency, then the value of the local currency will fluctuate in accordance with the value of the official currency.

Using Inventories as Reserves

One approach toward issuing a funded currency would be to use the value of inventories as the basis of issue. Since inventories must be maintained as part of the process of doing business anyway, why not use the value of those inventories to provide a sound medium of exchange? Basic commodities in inventory would seem to serve this purpose very well since they provide foundational inputs upon which subsequent economic activity depends, and provide an early indicator of value on the way to market. They would provide a medium of exchange which is grounded in reality and subject to all the natural limitations of the physical commodities which that exchange medium represents. The supply of money thus created would be self-regulating, expanding and contracting in step with changes in the stocks of the basic commodities.

One might envision such a currency being issued through a network of local merchant banks or business associations. The system would be decentralized, locally controlled, open, and subject to audit by a public-service, non-governmental agency. This is how it might work.

Newly produced grain, for example, might be deposited in a warehouse and new currency would be issued to the farmer in return for his warehouse receipt. The farmer would then be able to spend this money into circulation. When the grain is finally sold, to say, a miller, the miller would use money acquired in the market to buy the warehouse receipt allowing him to take possession of the grain. That money then would be extinguished. Having done its job, it is taken out of circulation. The process is shown pictorially in Figure 13.1.

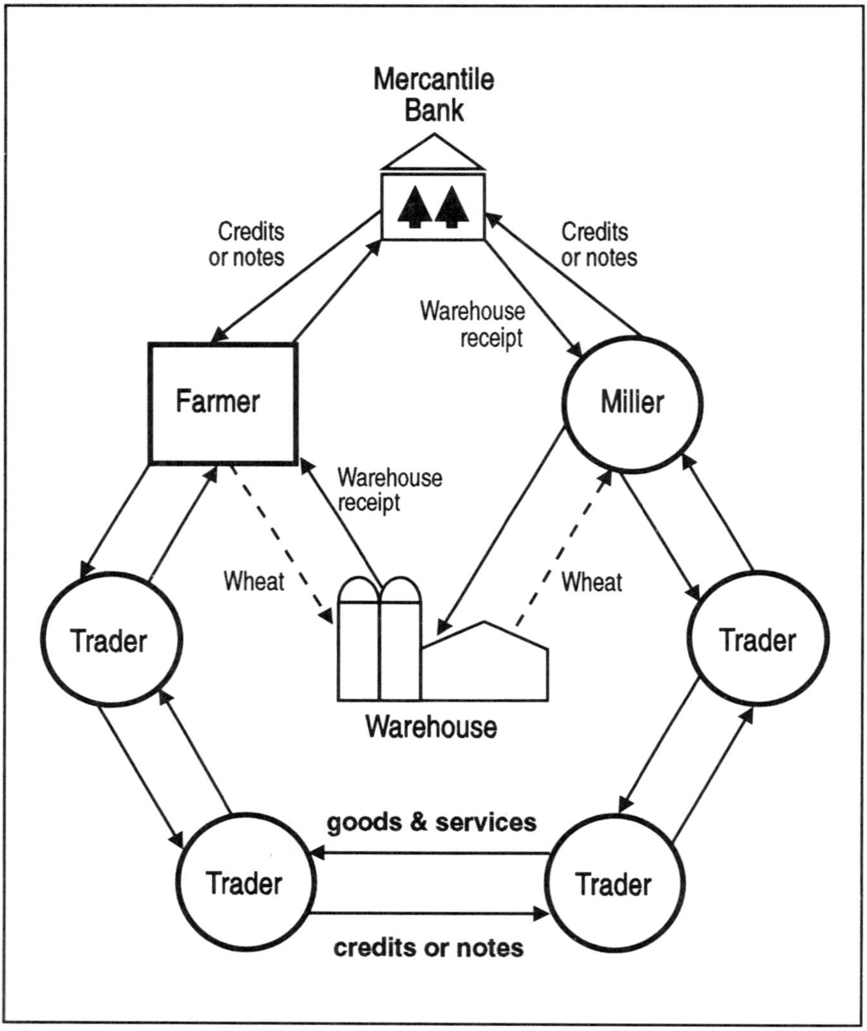

Figure 13.1: A Commodity-based Currency Circuit

Note that the warehouse receipt makes a complete circuit. It is issued by the warehouse to the farmer when he deposits wheat in the warehouse. The farmer then exchanges the receipt for credits or currency notes at the mercantile bank. The miller buys it from the mercantile bank using credits or notes which he has acquired in the course of doing business.

He then takes the receipt to the warehouse that originally issued it, where he exchanges it for the actual wheat. The warehouse receipt, having done its job, and having arrived back at its point of origin, is destroyed.

Likewise, the credits or notes also make a complete circuit. The mercantile bank creates and issues them to the farmer in exchange for his warehouse receipt. The farmer then spends them into circulation, in effect, exchanging them in trade for goods or services. They may subsequently be used by any number of traders to mediate exchanges of goods and/or services. Eventually, they are returned to the mercantile bank where they originated, and used to redeem the warehouse receipt which was the basis for their issuance. Once this basis is gone from the bank, the notes or credits must be retired.

In the present system, the supply of money is <u>not</u> automatically expanded to provide the means for purchasing the goods being brought to market. Since the supply of money may be artificially restricted, as well as misallocated, increased production typically drives market prices down. This causes producers to produce less, even though the real need and demand for the product may be far from being satisfied. This is one reason why there is hunger amidst plenty; many of those needing the food lack the money to buy it. If the need is there, and the supply is there, the money to match them up should also be there.

The current system makes producers slaves to money. There are three factors which create this condition. First, because money can only come into circulation through borrowing, a producer, one who owns real wealth, is allowed to convert that wealth to money only by becoming a debtor and using that wealth as collateral. Secondly, because interest is levied on this debt, most of the value, over time, is transferred to non-producers who control the money and banking process. Thirdly, because the supply of money is artificially regulated and kept in short supply relative to the amount needed for payments of the debt, some producers will inevitably default on their loans and be forced to forfeit their collateral.

Using basic commodities as the basis for issuing currency to producers automatically in proportion to their production makes the producer "king" by placing the money issuing power in his/her hands. It allows him/her to reap his proper reward for his contribution to the community. It creates the amount of currency necessary to allow the purchase of the goods produced -- the greater the amount produced, the greater the amount of currency in circulation; the more real wealth the community has (in the form of grain, lumber, metals, fuels, etc.), the more money there will be. Thus, the real wealth of the community is reflected (symbolically) in the amount of money in circulation.

If next year's production falls short of this year's, the amount of money retired in the process of redemption of commodities will be greater than the amount of new money issued. This will cause the money supply to contract along with the supply of commodities, reflecting the relative poverty of the community. If, on the other hand, production should increase from one period to the next, the amount of newly issued money will exceed the amount retired in the process of redemption. The supply of money will thus increase along with the supply of commodities, reflecting the relative prosperity of the community. This approach to currency issue would maintain a stable general price level, since there would be no central-bank-created artificial shortage, no legalized counterfeit from monetized government debt, no interest, and no misallocated bank credit.

Producers would not be charged interest on money issued in this manner. The initial amount of money issued on the strength of any particular warehouse receipt would be based upon the price history, stability of supply and perishability of the commodity. The final total received by the producer would be determined by the eventual price which he received in the market. Producers' accounts would be updated periodically to bring them into line with the actual market results.

An Example

To illustrate how this might work, consider an example of a wheat farmer. Suppose the recent history of wheat prices shows them to be fairly stable at around $3 a bushel. Farmer brings in a crop of 20,000 bushels of wheat which he deposits in a bonded warehouse. Upon receiving his warehouse receipt, Farmer takes it to the local cooperative mercantile bank which credits his account or gives him currency at full parity with the recent average price of $3.00.[97] Farmer thus receives $60,000 in currency or credit ($3 x 20,000). Now since wheat is perishable, Farmer is not going to wait too long to market it, if he can help it. Wheat has a limited storage life and proper storage costs money. The longer he waits, the greater his costs and the more the wheat deteriorates. Unless there is an upward fluctuation in the market price sufficient to offset them, these costs will result in Farmer getting a lower eventual total return.

Suppose Farmer sells his crop two weeks later for a price of $3.20 a bushel or a total of $64,000. His account will then be adjusted by adding the extra $4,000 which his crop proved to be worth over the $60,000 originally issued to him. In the unlikely event that the coop bank were to badly misjudge the market and Farmer could only get $2.60 for his wheat, his account would be debited for the difference of $8,000. If his account balance was insufficient to cover the debit it could be carried over and Farmer would receive that much less when his next crop was deposited.

Now suppose Miller buys the wheat from Farmer for $3.20 a bushel or a total of $64,000. Miller must then take that amount of currency to the bank. Of that amount, $4,000 is credited to Farmer's account and the remaining $60,000 is used to redeem the warehouse receipt. Miller then takes the warehouse receipt to the warehouse, which allows him to withdraw the wheat. The warehouse receipt is then canceled. Since the bank no longer has the warehouse receipt, the $60,000 which Miller paid to redeem it must go out of circulation.[98] When both the warehouse

---

[97] Some might argue that some amount less than full parity should be credited, say 80%. This, however, would place into circulation an amount of money insufficient to purchase the deposited commodity at par, thus tending to force prices down and preventing the producer from obtaining an adequate return or recovering his/her costs.

[98] In actual practice, the details of the procedure might be somewhat different but the effect would be as described. The bank, which maintains a continuous inventory record and issues release certificates for withdrawal of

receipt and the credits or notes which were issued on its basis have made the complete circuit, they are then retired. The process begins again when more wheat or other valuable commodities are deposited in the warehouse.

Under this type of system, nobody has to go into debt to bring money into circulation, the amount of money and the amount of value are always in balance, and there is a natural incentive to expedite commerce and keep the money circulating rapidly. There are two reasons for this. First, it is to the farmer's advantage to sell his crop quickly to avoid storage costs and spoilage. Secondly, it is to his/her advantage to spend his/her money into circulation, giving others the means to buy his crop. All that one need do to issue money under such a system is to be productive.

---

wheat from the warehouse, would begin to retire currency from circulation as it came in to pay for the wheat. This is somewhat similar to existing bank practice with regard to financing automobile dealers' inventories of vehicles, except that banks charge substantial interest.

CHAPTER 14 COMMUNITY TRADING COUPONS

"Change occurs when there is a confluence of both changing values and economic necessity, not before."

-- John Naisbitt[99]

Bootstrapping The Local Economy

Everybody knows how discount coupons work -- 10% off, 20% off, 2-for-1, $1 off, etc. -- and every business operator knows that coupons can boost sales. But, even though a well-designed coupon campaign can stimulate business, it is not without its own costs. First, there is the cost of designing the coupon, then the cost of getting it into the hands of the potential customer, and finally, the lost revenue of the discount itself. The hope, of course, is that these costs will be more than made up for by the increased business which the coupons generate, but that may or may not result. As competing businesses adopt the coupon strategy, its effectiveness tends to diminish and profit margins may be permanently reduced for everyone.

One of the primary factors which makes the use of coupons and other gimmicks necessary, even more than the local competitive climate, is the general deficiency of money in circulation. This is especially true during periods of so-called "recession." But even under "normal" economic conditions, the customers of a particular type of business may have their buying potential restricted because their disposable income is not keeping pace with inflation. This deficiency of money in circulation derives generally, not from any inadequacy in the resources or productive capacity of the local economy, but rather from the workings of remote agencies, including The Federal Reserve Board, the Federal government, large commercial banks, and the central banks of other countries. These agencies, which are closely inter-linked and often act in consort, hold tight control over the media of exchange, and by their policies, which they pursue in their own interests, can stimulate or strangle both national and local economies.

As we have pointed out, however, there are local initiatives which can be used to effectively preserve the integrity of local economies in the

---

[99] Naisbitt, John, *Megatrends*. New York: Warner Books, 1982, p. 183

face of adverse external conditions; initiatives which are private, voluntary, and do not depend upon government-granted privileges. One such strategy involves the issuance of coupons. There is a way for local businesses to get all of the benefits of a coupon campaign without having to incur most of the usual costs. They can do this if they will cooperate as well as compete.

Suppose a group of businesses decided to cooperate in jointly issuing coupons which they all would agree to accept, not only from the public, but from each other, as well. Let's say that each business would agree to accept payment partly in cash and partly in coupons, with each business itself deciding what percentage of the price to accept in coupons. This percentage could be based on the costs and value-added of the particular business (subject to some minimum percentage), allowing cash costs to be met, while all or part of the value added by a business would be received in coupon form. The percentage of the purchase price which each business is willing to accept in Coupons would be advertised and posted on the premises. As an example, Primo Pizzeria might advertise, "We accept Community Trading Coupons for up to 30% of the purchase price on any pizza." Of course, those accepting a higher percentage of payment in coupons would probably attract more of the available business than those accepting a lower percentage. Such a coupon might look like the one pictured in Figure 14.1.

Now how exactly would these coupons be issued? This is the key question. It must be done properly to keep the coupons circulating and in demand. The primary factor here is the nature of the agreement among the cooperating merchants. It must be carefully formulated, clearly stated, and adhered to. Ideally, it should be enforced, not by any outside authority or by resort to the legal system, but by the parties to the agreement themselves. Given a well-developed agreement, the opportunity for continued participation should by itself be adequate incentive for adhering to its terms.

Here's one way it could work. The cooperative group could issue standardized, pre-printed coupon blanks to each member business, in any amount desired, up to the equivalent of 2 month's potential average

1 Community Trading Coupon 1

This coupon will be accepted in trade by any participating merchant, on any purchase, for up to the merchant's posted percentage of the purchase price.

1 SUPPORT YOUR LOCAL ECONOMY 1

Figure 14.1: Conceptual Rendering of a Community Trading Coupon

coupon receipts from sales. Thus, a business having average monthly sales of $20,000, which agrees to accept 20% of payment in coupons, could be issued up to $8,000 worth of coupon blanks:

> $20,000 monthly sales x 2 months x 20% payment in coupons = $8,000.

Similarly, a business having average monthly sales of $40,000, which agrees to accept 50% of payment in coupons, could be issued up to $40,000 worth of coupon blanks:

> $40,000 monthly sales x 2 months x 50% payment in coupons = $40,000.

The recipient business could then "spend" these coupons on purchases it makes from any other member businesses. It would, by accepting the blank coupons from the cooperative, obligate itself to redeem, *i.e.* give back to the cooperative, an equal amount of coupons over some period of time.

If the coupons have a limited life, this would force their redemption to take place within some finite time period. Of course, any business which is a member in good standing could be issued new coupons for the old ones which it redeemed, maintaining the circulation of coupons generally. Members would also agree that, if and when they wish to

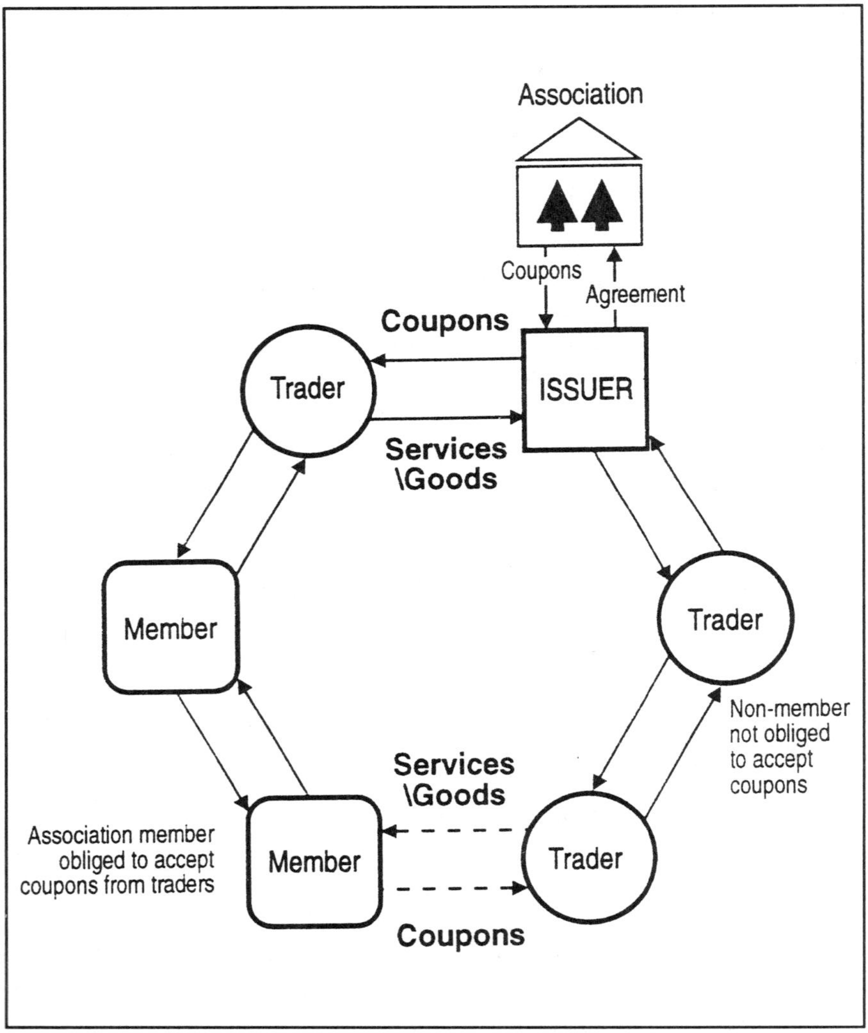

Figure 14.2: The Community Trading Coupon Circuit

withdraw from the cooperative, they would turn over the same amount of coupons they originally received, and make up any deficiency using official currency.

Some coupons will inevitably be lost or fail to be redeemed by the expiration date. This amount can be credited to an "insurance and public benefit fund" which would be used to cover losses due to bankruptcy or default of some members. Any accumulated amount, over and above that needed for prudent insurance of losses, could be used to support the cooperative itself or be donated to local non-profit community-improvement organizations. The cooperative might also impose certain levies upon its members for these purposes.

A coupon would first enter circulation when a member "spends" it on a purchase. The spender would validate the coupon by signing and/or stamping it, and dating it (or dates could be pre-printed on the coupons). The recipient of the coupon could then, in turn, spend it on purchases from any other member of the cooperative, <u>or anyone else willing to accept it in payment.</u> Thus, the coupons could circulate as a supplemental medium of exchange up to their expiration date, the holder being assured that they would be accepted, at least, by all the members of the cooperative. This process is depicted in Figure 14.2.

The benefits to the member businesses should be apparent. Instead of competing with each other for whatever scarce official money might be circulating within the community, they would be cooperating to supplement that money with a local exchange medium, making it possible to transact a greater amount of trade. Since the coupons would have value only for purchases made locally, they would remain in the community instead of being used to buy from outside the community, tending to make it more self-reliant and less dependent upon imports from outside. Since anyone would be allowed to spend them, their use would benefit not only the members of the cooperative but everyone in the community. As the member businesses begin to thrive, others will be inclined to accept the coupons also, causing the amount in circulation to increase, and giving the community greater control over its own economic life.

CHAPTER 15 GOOD MONEY FOR GOOD WORK

"Our objective should be to create exchange media issued on the basis of human service and Earth service rather than acquisitiveness and domination."

-- Greco

In addressing the mega-crisis which confronts the world today, it should be clear that decisive changes will need to be made in the methods we humans use to distribute power and allocate material resources. As pointed out earlier, the present dominant structures of money and finance, by their very nature, promote the concentration of power into fewer and fewer hands, increase the disparity in the distribution of wealth, channel the vast majority of the earth's resources into wasteful production, and force both social and ecological degradation. The pinnacle of power today is the power to issue money. If that power can be democratized and focused in a direction which gives social and ecological concerns top priority, then there may yet be hope for saving the world.

This chapter describes three proposals for achieving that. These proposals have two primary features: (1) the use of local currencies to facilitate trade and (2) the empowerment of groups which are working to serve the common good. Although they are described in terms of circulating certificates or notes, these exchange media could also take the form of credits in a mutual credit system or some combination of account credits and circulating notes.

The basis of issue of money has, in times past, been more neutral than at present. Now, with the issuance of money controlled by the central government/central bank nexus, it has become a mechanism by which these elements control the application of human and capital resources and allocate them to projects which are usually self-serving, wasteful of resources, and often downright destructive. Our objective should be to create exchange media issued on the basis of human service and Earth service rather than acquisitiveness and domination.

The exchange media described below put control of the exchange process into the hands of the people, giving them more choice over how they will apply their energies and resources. The willingness of others in the community to accept the new exchange media in payment for goods and services, especially the necessities of life, does two things -- it encourages the application of people's energies and resources to life-sustaining activities, and it provides the community with a medium of exchange that by its very nature is abundant, democratic, and locally controlled.

Earth Rescue Receipts (ERR's)

Earth Rescue Receipts (ERR's) are paper receipts for contributions made to what we will call "good work" organizations. ERR's would be issued by any organization which is a member of a consortium of mutual aid, social action, community improvement, environmental and other such organizations. These receipts, issued in small denominations, would simply acknowledge the donation of money, materials, equipment or services to a member organization. They would provide evidence that the donor has done "good work." Unlike the usual receipt form used to acknowledge a donation or payment, ERR's would be printed in standardized denominations, say $5, $10, $20, and $50, and would bear the name and seal of the consortium. When a donor makes a donation, the receipt would be dated and signed and/or validated by the recipient organization and given to the donor. Such a receipt might look like the one shown in Figure 15.1.

Except for the standard denominations, the steps described above are much the same as current practice. So what are the key features of the ERR proposal which make it empowering? Well, what if the donor, who now holds the ERR, were able to get something of value for it? Suppose some local businesses were to agree to accept ERR's in trade? In that case, ERR's could become a circulating currency. The original donor would not be any poorer for having made the donation, but would simply have "gotten the ball rolling." An ERR would be considered to be a "temporary receipt" (TR) which could be spent. Thus, ERR's would pass from hand to hand, enabling any number of trades.

Anyone wishing to make a permanent donation would take ERR's to any organization which is a consortium member and exchange them for a

10 Earth Rescue Receipt 10

This coupon is evidence that a contribution of 10 dollars has been made to a member organization of the Community Improvement Consortium. It may be circulated as currency or it may be exchanged for a permanent tax receipt when donated to any member organization.

Signed ____________________ Date ________

Support your local economy; accept ERR's in trade

10 FOR EARTH AND COMMUNITY 10

Figure 15.1: Conceptual Rendering of an Earth Rescue Receipt

"permanent receipt" (PR) which s/he would hold for tax purposes.[100] This is the means by which ERR's would be extinguished and go out of circulation. If at any point in time there were an excess of ERR's in circulation (as evidenced by discounting or refusal of ERR's in the marketplace), the consortium would suspend further issuance until permanent donations caught up with temporary donations and reduced the amount of ERR's in circulation to the proper level. Figure 15.2 is a pictorial illustration which shows the process of issuance, circulation, and redemption of Earth Rescue Receipts.

As the positive effects of this process become more evident, more and more people will want to share the burden of community improvement, either by making additional donations to the member organizations, or

---

[100] As I understand it, the IRS currently does not recognize the donation of services as a tax-deductible contribution. Only cash and in-kind donations qualify. Some change in the tax regulations might be necessary to gain tax advantages for donation of ERR's.

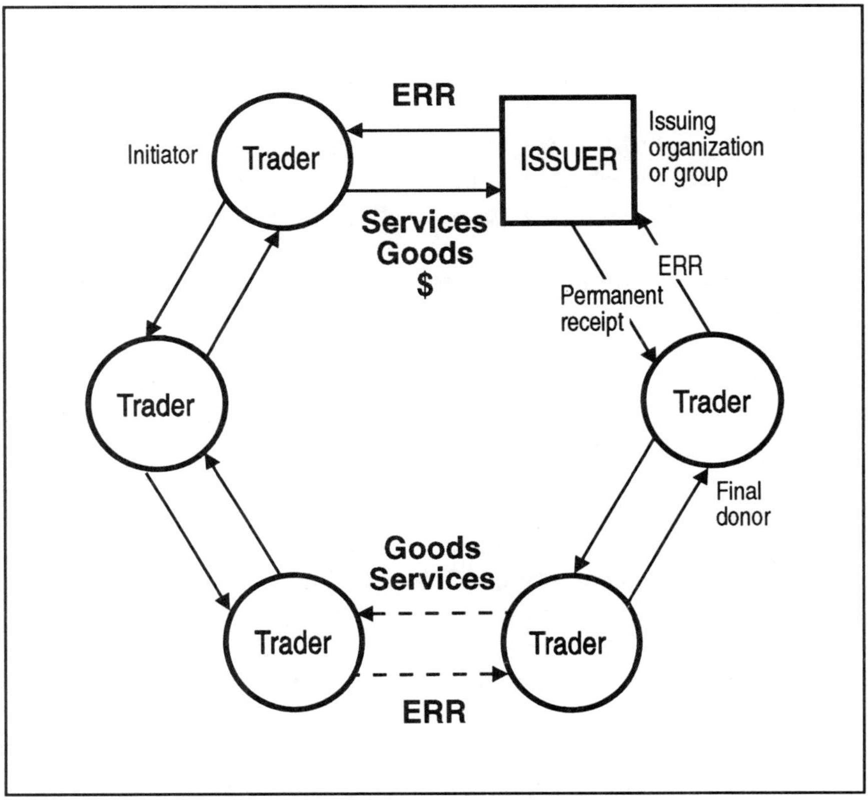

Figure 15.2: The Earth Rescue Receipt Circuit

by accepting ERR's in trade and in the payment of debts. Growing acceptance of this exchange medium, and the increasing local prosperity which it brings, will encourage greater and greater amounts to be contributed to the "good work" organizations and encourage work which is in the public interest. As the use of ERR's expands and proliferates, this process could largely replace taxation as a means of supporting the common good. Besides providing a local medium of exchange, it would provide a more participatory process for local community finance, eliminating the need for many government expenditures and transfer payments.

Questions and Answers:

1. Q. Why would anyone accept Earth Rescue Receipts instead of official currency?
A. ERR's will be acceptable for three reasons:
ERR's will appeal, first to those who support the activities which give rise to their issuance; secondly, to those who can see the benefits which a local currency provides in strengthening the local economy; and thirdly to those who can see that they represent a sound medium of exchange which is spendable in the community.

2. Q. What will make ERR's a sound medium of exchange?
A. ERR's are not issued arbitrarily. They are issued on the basis of actual contributions of value to a participating organization. Each ERR, therefore, represents a receipt for actual value delivered, either in cash, materials, labor or services. The amount of ERR's issued can never exceed the amount of value delivered. An ERR will circulate only until some holder decides to contribute it back to an issuing organization. At that point a permanent receipt will be issued to the donor, to be held for tax purposes, and the ERR will be retired from circulation until a new donation makes it possible to reissue it.

3. Q. Suppose not enough ERR's are donated back to member organizations, won't the amount in circulation keep building up and cause inflation?[101]
A. That's an excellent question and it gets to the heart of the monetary problem. The issuance of ERR's, or any other currency which people are free to discount or refuse, can never cause inflation. Here's why. First of all, one must understand what inflation is. Inflation is an increase in the general level of prices expressed in terms of the predominant currency unit - in the present case, Federal Reserve "dollars." In the past, the unit of account which we use, the dollar, was defined as a particular weight of gold. Paper notes were issued to represent gold dollars and were

---

[101] This topic was fully covered in Chapter 9.

convertible, on demand of the holder, into gold, at the bank. When paper notes or bank credits are improperly issued into circulation, the value of all such notes is diluted; people will then prefer to hold gold instead of paper. If they accept paper at all, it will be at a discount, *i.e.* they might accept paper dollar notes but ask a higher price in paper dollars than in gold dollars.

When money is an object of political control, as it has become in every country of the world, the issuing authorities will attempt to prevent the discounting of their notes and the loss of their gold reserves by redemption. They will refuse to convert the paper currency into gold and declare the notes to be "legal tender." The effect of these measures is to obliterate the value standard and force acceptance of the inferior paper currency. When this happens, sellers have no way of protecting themselves from harm except by raising prices. Without a forced acceptance of the currency, there can be no inflation. Thus, inflation, which consists of higher prices generally, is really a symptom that the market is devaluing the official currency. Since traders are required by law to accept it at face value, the only adjustment they can make is to raise their prices.

So the answer to your question is that, since ERR's need not be accepted at face value, an excess of ERR's in circulation will cause them to be discounted or refused by sellers in the market. If people see this happening, they will tend to ease off on making initial donations of goods and services because the ERR's they would receive could not be spent for full value. At the other end of the line, permanent donors who can make use of the tax deduction will tend to accept more ERR's to donate for tax purposes since they can acquire ERR's more cheaply. For example, if a one dollar ERR is being accepted in the market at only 90 cents, a permanent donor could obtain a $1 tax deduction at a cost of only 90 cents. Whenever the market is free to discount the value of a note (accept it at less than face value), this fact makes that currency system self-adjusting.

So to sum up, what can happen with an alternative currency is that it might not be accepted at par with the unit of account or official currency. In the past, discounting of private currencies below par has occurred. Such discounting is the result of improper issuance. In the case of Earth Rescue Receipts, the amount issued is strictly determined by the amount of value already donated, which itself is a measure of the community's willingness to support the activities of the issuing organizations.

The deciding factor on the amount which will remain in circulation is the time period within which the receipts will be deemed to be valid in trade. This could be six months, a year, or forever. If an expiration date is specified, an ERR would no longer be accepted in trade after that date, but the holder could still exchange it for a permanent receipt and obtain the associated tax deduction. The experience of the market should make the determination as to whether or not an expiration date should be used.

4. Q. How will counterfeiting be avoided?
A. Effective anti-counterfeiting measures have been well developed over a period of many years. These are commonly employed by governments and issuing banks to protect their currencies. They involve close security over the printing process, special inks and papers, serial numbering, and other measures. There is no reason why these same measures cannot be utilized for local currencies. Beyond that, there are two additional factors which will discourage counterfeiting of a local currency. The limited area within which they are accepted and limited time period within which they would be circulated as a payment medium tend to make counterfeiting unprofitable.

Funded Temporary Receipts (FTR's)

While a local currency system such as the Earth Rescue Receipts described above might approach more closely the ideals for monetary transformation set forth previously, a funded local currency might be initially more acceptable and less vulnerable to official interference. It would probably provide better tax advantages to donors under current

IRS regulations. It would be similar in many ways to the Earth Rescue Receipts and could work as follows:

1. A consortium of non-profit, social action and community improvement groups could begin a program under which a trustee would accept, on behalf of its members as a group, deposits of official money from any benefactor.

2. These deposits would constitute an endowment fund which would be invested in ways which would provide income in official currency to help the organizations meet their cash needs. It might be wise to invest these funds only in direct obligations of the U.S. Treasury, *i.e.* government bills, notes and bonds.[102] Alternatively, the funds might be invested in securities of quasi-governmental agencies such as the Government National Mortgage Association (GNMA) and Federal Farm Credit Bank, which might use them in more socially responsible ways.

3. These deposits would be non-refundable to the depositor; instead, the consortium would issue to the depositor "funded temporary receipts" (FTR's) in standard small denominations, say $5, $10, $20, and $50. FTR's would bear the name and seal of the consortium.

4. These FTR's would be spendable with any business or individual willing to accept them.

5. FTR's would thus circulate as currency.

---

[102] Although United States currency is presently issued by the Federal Reserve banking cartel, the U.S. government is its ultimate guarantor. U.S. Treasury bills, notes and bonds represent direct obligations of the U.S. Government and are the ultimate in safety, even in these shaky times. Their safety derives from the power of the government to impose taxes on the people. Fall they may, but they will likely be among the last securities to do so. In the meantime, they provide a safe store of value, plus interest income which can be used to bolster "good work" organizations. Since U.S. Government securities provide the basis for much of the money issued by the banks, there is a certain elegance about using the same securities to establish a new transformational exchange medium.

6. Any individual wishing to make a permanent contribution to any member organization of the consortium could do so by delivering FTR's to that organization.

7. The organization would then issue to the donor a permanent receipt (PR) for tax purposes, allowing the donor to receive a tax deduction for his/her contribution.

8. Such contributions would certainly be tax-deductible because they represent the final action in conveying to the recipient organization entitlement to the deposit of official money.[103]

9. Only recipient organizations which are members of the "good work" consortium would be allowed to redeem the temporary receipts for official currency (draw official money out of the endowment pool), and only to a limited extent, preserving most or all of the principal and allowing only the income to be spent.[104]

10. Interest earned on the Treasury investments would accrue to the consortium and be credited to the members' accounts in proportion to the amount in "funded temporary receipts" donated to each organization in the given period. Thus, the organizations which are most strongly supported by the community will receive the greater portion of the investment earnings, as well.

11. Organizations which are consortium members need not use the temporary receipts (FTR's) which they receive as donations to draw official money out of the pool, but instead may choose to spend them

---

[103] Donations of services, on the other hand, are not deductible under current IRS regulations.

[104] Ideally, there should be no liquidation of the security fund at all. As the pool of government securities increases, more official money would be replaced with FTRs, transforming the medium of exchange from a debt-based medium to a service-based medium. As a practical matter though, the interest income from the endowment fund would probably be distributed to member organizations to help meet their cash needs.

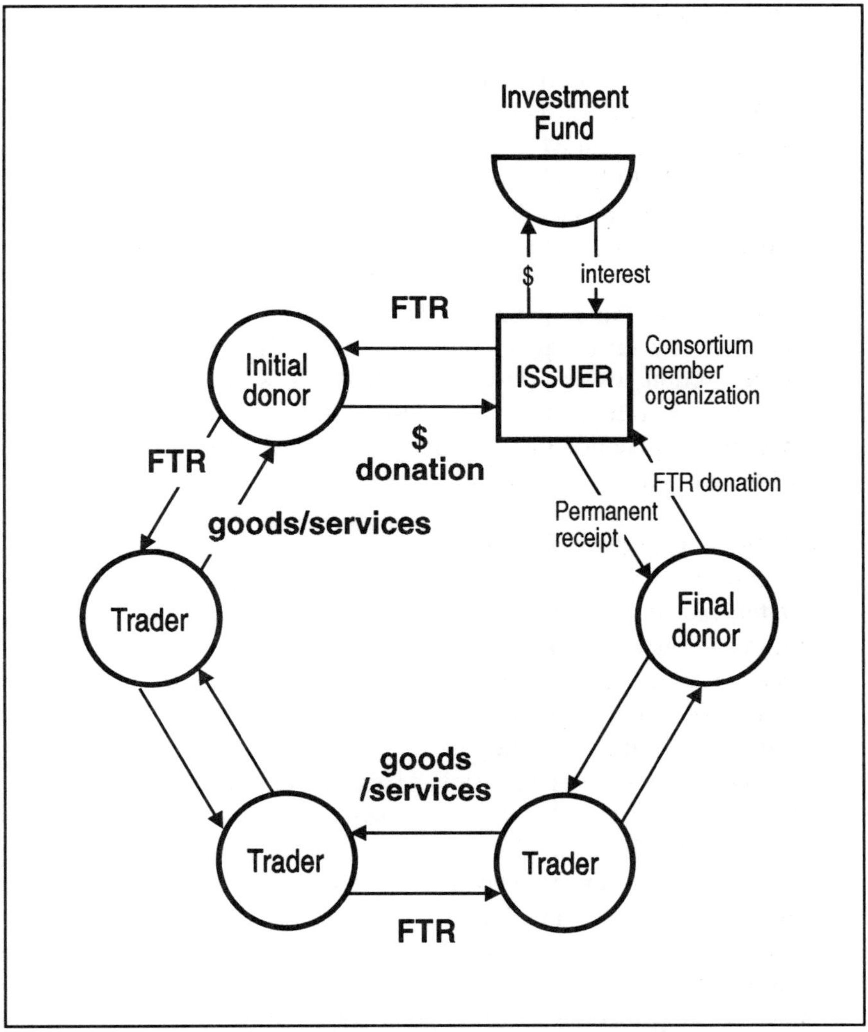

Figure 15.3: The Funded Temporary Receipt (FTR) Circuit

back into circulation, using them to pay employees and suppliers. Likewise, any interest income credited to its account, instead of being withdrawn in dollar currency, could be left on deposit and used as the basis for spending an equivalent amount of FTR's into circulation. Figure 15.3 is a pictorial illustration of the process.

Questions and Answers:

1. Q. What's the point of this project?
A. There are several beneficial results which can be expected from the implementation of this project. The main objective though is to shift the bulk of human effort away from conspicuous consumption, waste and the production of war materiel, toward "good work" which addresses human needs and the needs of the planet.

2. Q. How does this plan achieve that?
A. First, by encouraging the support of organizations which are taking action toward positive change, and secondly, by partially substituting a democratic, locally-controlled, asset-based exchange medium in place of the official monopolized, centrally-controlled, debt-based exchange medium.

3. Q. Well, how does that work?
A. It encourages the support of "good work" organizations by reason of the fact that the original depositor need not necessarily be the ultimate donor, but s/he may be able to spend the FTR's which s/he receives in return for making a deposit. The process of donation is begun when the deposit is made and temporary receipts (FTR's) issued, but completed only when the FTR's are delivered by the ultimate donor back to some participating organization. Thus, anyone with a dollar can "get the ball rolling" without making any financial sacrifice at all, except to forego the potential interest income on the money deposited. But if a donor is relatively poor and needs to spend the money instead of investing it anyway, this represents no loss to him/her. Yet, it does result in a gain for the consortium group. In effect, the official currency becomes a capital pool earning income for the "good work" organizations; even the poor are empowered to be philanthropic; and the community is provided with a democratic, locally controlled, life-supporting medium of exchange.

   This approach could ultimately transform the entire official money supply into an endowment fund for good work. Further, it allows the supporters of good work, as a group, to maximize their collective tax advantage. Those who can make the best use of the tax deduction will be the ones who make the ultimate donations (of FTR's).

In the existing system of money and finance, money is first allocated to those enterprises which promise the greatest monetary return, or to those mandated by the existing power structure -- mega-corporations, government bureaucracies, military establishments, land and corporate speculators. Under the proposed system, the allocation priorities are reversed. It puts positive change and public service groups first instead of last in the allocation of funds, and empowers the realization of popular values, not just those of the rich and powerful. It may help to fulfill the prediction that "...(the) first shall be last, and the last first."[105]

4. Q. Can other organizations join the consortium after it is initially formed?
   A. Yes. Any organization wishing to participate may be admitted to the consortium by agreeing to the terms of membership.

5. Q. What if an organization is philosophically opposed to those already in it?
   A. In the spirit of conviviality, no non-profit organization should be excluded. Nor are exclusionary qualifications necessary because an organization can directly benefit only to the extent that people make donations of FTR's to it. Thus, membership in the consortium in itself does not provide any direct financial benefit to an organization; it benefits only to the extent that it has popular support and receives donations of FTR's.

---

[105] Mark 10:31.

Cooperative Community Service Credits

A Cooperative Community Service Credit system provides another way of mobilizing resources to serve community needs. It too is similar to the Earth Rescue Receipt, but focuses more specifically on volunteer services and specific projects. There is always a limit to the amount of time and energy which volunteers can afford to donate. A service credit system attempts to transcend the limitations of reliance upon volunteer service by acknowledging the value of services rendered, without the payment of scarce money, but by issuing service credit receipts.

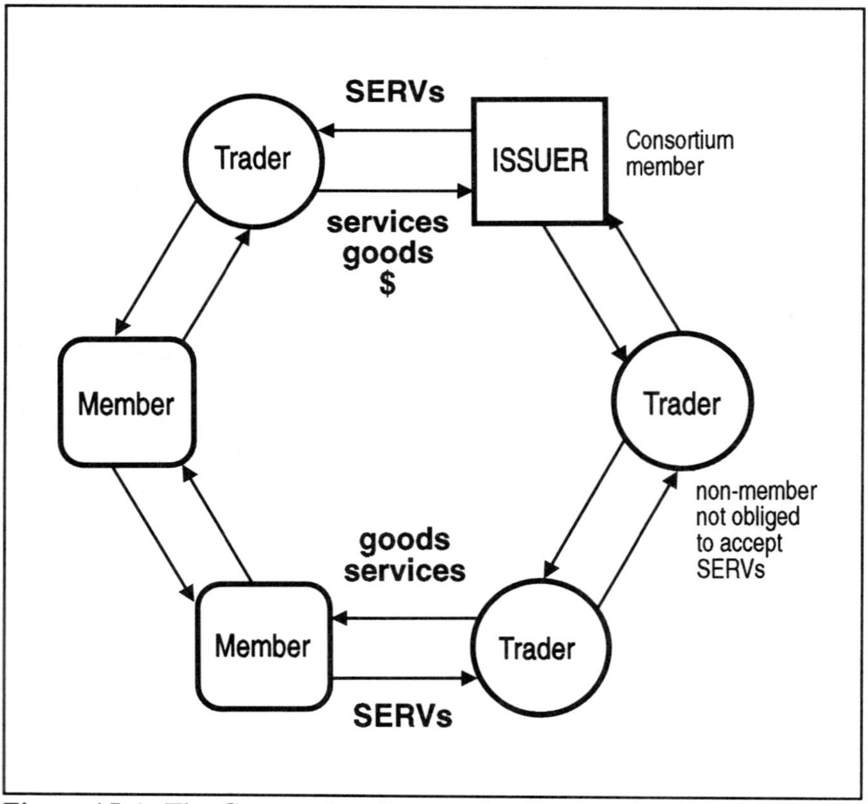

Figure 15.4: The Cooperative Community Service Credit (SERV) Circuit

Businesses, as well as individuals, in the community could be encouraged to accept service credits in partial or full payment for the goods and services they offer for sale. The issuing organization(s), then, would accept the receipts from others either as donations or in payment for some of the services it provides.

How it Might Work

Let's consider a possible example. Let's call the value unit in this system a "SERV." A SERV would be equivalent to one dollar's worth of service. A group of social action, community, environmental, self-help, and mutual-aid organizations might agree to jointly publish a periodical for education and outreach. All work would be paid in service credit receipts (SERVS) redeemable by the publication for copy space in the publication, advertising, and other related services, such as typesetting, layout, mailing list management, etc. The more space a member organization wants in the magazine, the more service credit receipts it must deliver to the consortium. It can get them as donations, or earn them by doing work on the publication, or by selling some of its services. Figure 15.4 shows the creation and circulation of Cooperative Community Service Credits.

Businesses can earn SERVS by accepting them in trade, either from the individuals who have earned them by working on the publication, or from other businesses which have accepted them in payment. The businesses can then donate the receipts to any member organization, or use them to pay for advertising in the publication. Businesses, by accepting the receipts in partial payment for their goods and services, would stimulate their own business just as the use of a discount coupon does, but unlike a discount coupon, service credit receipts can be passed along (spent) for value, or donated to promote activities of benefit to the community. Such a system might be started by making an announcement like the following.

ANNOUNCEMENT

YOUR CHANCE TO SUPPORT A HEALTHY COMMUNITY AND A CLEAN ENVIRONMENT

ANNOUNCING PUBLICATION OF THE *COMMUNITY WEEKLY*

All of our workers are paid for their work in "service credits," or "SERVS." You can support them and our publication by accepting our service credit receipts as you would your own discount coupons, for, say 20%, 30%, 50%, or more, off your regular prices. But, unlike discount coupons, service credit receipts can be used by you to buy things you need. You yourself can spend SERVS for goods and services offered by other participating businesses, or you can use them to buy valuable advertising in our magazine, *COMMUNITY WEEKLY*. You can also use SERVS to pay for our typesetting, design, and layout services. We can do your advertising flyers, menus, business cards, or forms. Or, you might prefer to donate SERVS to any of our member organizations which you might wish to support.

Call today and let us add you to our list of participating businesses. We will periodically publish this list in our magazine, indicating for each business, the percentage of payment which it accepts in SERVS. The higher the percentage, the more business you'll attract. And remember, it costs you nothing, because you, in turn, can spend the SERVS you accept. By accepting *COMMUNITY WEEKLY* service credits, you'll be helping the magazine to improve the community and you'll be boosting your own business. EVERYBODY WINS!

Each business would sign an agreement form such as the one below:

___(Name of business)___ agrees to accept ___(Name of consortium/publication)___ service credit receipts (SERVS) in partial payment for all products and services which it offers, to the extent of _____% of the purchase price. ___(Name of consortium/publication)__ agrees to accept its own service credit receipts at face value in payment for advertising or other services which it customarily offers, to the extent of _____% of its standard fees.

This agreement may be canceled by either party at any time upon written notice.

Signed___________________________ Date________

Signed___________________________ Date________

CHAPTER 16 A MODEL COMPOSITE LOCAL EXCHANGE SYSTEM

Any sizeable group anywhere, any day, could start a nonpolitical monetary unit and system. There is no law against it, and no legislation need be invoked.

-- E. C. Riegel[106]

My work with LETSonora, the cashless trading system in southeastern Arizona, has provided an opportunity to experiment with various approaches and system enhancements. Although there is no single community exchange model which I consider to be adequate, there are several which contain useful elements. If we keep in mind the fundamental principles of equity, freedom and inclusiveness, and equip ourselves with sound theoretical knowledge, we can continue our approach toward an ideal exchange system. I am presently inclined to favor a composite system which incorporates several of the ideas discussed in previous chapters. Given the current state of the art in the development of complementary exchange systems, I would recommend that a local exchange system be established according to the following guidelines:

1. Organize the system as a non-profit organization (it need not be legally incorporated, but larger operations should be).

2. Allow membership to be open to include individuals, non-profit organizations, and businesses.

3. Organize the system as a mutual credit system, but provide for the use of circulating notes, coupons, or receipts as an option to the transfer of credits through the ledger accounts.

4. Avoid charging interest on debit balances. Service charges should be fixed amounts based on the cost of the services rendered. If system charges are levied against account balances, they should be assessed equally on **both** debit **and** credit balances.

---

[106] *Flight From Inflation. op.cit.*, p. 49.

5. Elect a Board of Overseers, whose powers are limited and clearly defined at the outset.

6. Establish credit (debit balance) limits for members according to a definite formula involving the member's average level of sales.

7. Do **not** provide the option of redemption of local currencies or credits in official currencies (dollars).

As has been stated previously, banking should be conducted as a profession, not run as a business for profit. To avoid conflicts of interest in the operation of a local exchange system, it should be established as a cooperative or mutual association, "owned" by its members and run entirely for the benefit of the community. Since membership is open to everyone, there should be no problem with regard to representing and safeguarding the public interest.

Many LETS systems, in which the membership has consisted of only individuals, have been slow to grow. While LETS membership is open to businesses, LETS systems have not generally been very successful in attracting them. I believe it is very important to make a concerted effort to include established businesses, as well as individual members, in the start-up of a local exchange system. Established businesses, in addition to their name recognition, offer a wider range of goods and services and a greater volume of trading. Since they already are significant players in the local economy, business members provide local exchange systems with the prospect of a faster start and greater impact. The success of *Ithaca HOURS* is, I believe, mainly due to the extensive participation of local businesses.

The Governing Board

A local exchange system, whether it be simply a ledger system, a paper currency issue, or some combination of the two, requires some administrative group or authority. It is very important that the administrative Board be constrained in its power. No matter how well intentioned the people might be, "power corrupts," as we have so often seen. That's the basic problem with the existing monetary and governmental structures. The Board should have very little discretion. Its function should be to establish the basic ground rules at the outset, monitor the members' adherence to their agreements, and take the appropriate prescribed action in the event they do not. The Board would provide application forms to prospective members and oversee the processing of applications, verifying the information upon which each member's participation and debit limits are based (specifically, his/her average monthly sales volume and cost of goods sold and/or value added).

Credit Limits for Members

One of the fundamental questions in a local exchange system is that of how much credit to authorize to each individual or business member, *i.e.*, how large a debit balance each member should be allowed to carry. For ease of discussion, let us refer to any unit of local trade credit as a "Riegel," after E.C. Riegel, one of the most lucid thinkers on the question of money. The number of Riegels or local trade units which a business or individual is expected to redeem in the course of trade each month should be the only basis for deciding the amount of credit to be authorized, and it should be based on a formula relationship such as the one described in a previous chapter. That formula is based on the following rationale:

1. The member business itself decides what percentage of each sale to accept in Riegels, based on its proportion of "value added." Thus, a business which has a cost of goods sold of 60% (gross margin of 40%) and a net profit margin of 20% of sales, could choose to accept a percentage of Riegels anywhere in between 20 and 40 percent, depending on how much of their administrative costs they expect to be able to pay for with Riegels. One might expect them to start with the lower figure to be safe, then increase it as experience merits. There is no apparent reason for the Board to have any say about this percentage.

2. Adherents of the "German school" have pointed out that a viable currency should have a 1% daily reflux. That means that the whole

volume of currency must flow back to the issuers within about a 100 day period. It might be prudent to agree, at least initially, to have a total reflux within a 60 day period. That means each member business could be authorized to issue an amount of Riegels up to the amount it would be expected to redeem in trade during an average 60 day period (2 months). That's a simple formula calculation:

Authorized Credit, Riegels =
(2 x monthly sales) x (Riegel payment percentage)

EXAMPLE

If a business has monthly sales of $80,000 and agrees to accept 20% payment in Riegels, it would be authorized to issue a total of 32,000 Riegels:

32,000 Riegels = (2 x $80,000) x (.20)

3. A member business should be allowed to adjust the percentage up or down as it sees fit, up to the limit of its value added percentage[107]. If up, it would be authorized to issue more Riegels in accordance with the formula. If a business ever wanted to decrease its percentage, or drop out completely, all it would need to do is repay the difference in the amount of Riegels it was authorized to issue. If it did not have enough Riegels to do that, it would have to earn them in trade, or it could be allowed to pay the remainder in any mutually agreed upon medium of exchange, presumably official currency.

Employee Participation

Employees of member businesses should be encouraged to become associate members. They would agree to accept a particular percentage of their wages in Riegels. In return, they might be allowed, themselves,

---

[107] This limit might eventually be relaxed or eliminated as the system becomes established and stable operation is demonstrated.

to issue (spend into circulation) an amount of Riegels computed in the same way as the business authorization is determined.

> EXAMPLE
>
> If an employee earning $1,000 a month agrees to accept 30% of her salary in Riegels, she could be allowed to issue (spend) up to a total of 600 Riegels. (She would also be getting 300 Riegels a month in her pay envelope, but these are Riegels she earns, not issues.)

Employees will, no doubt, want to jump on the bandwagon when they see the system working. As unemployment becomes more of a problem, and official money becomes less available, people will probably be willing to work for most any kind of money which they deem to be trustworthy. As we have seen in previous chapters, when there is not enough official currency circulating in the local economy, a local currency can put people to work and provide a means by which they can get their needs met.

Ledger Accounts or Paper Notes?

Conceptually, it doesn't matter whether the Riegels take the form of paper notes, tokens, or ledger balances (bookkeeping entries). These are all symbolic representations of the same thing -- the values being exchanged, and each is "backed" by the same commitment of the issuers to redeem them -- so checks and notes and electronic transfers can all be used interchangeably, as they are in the official monetary system.

Convertibility of Local Currency to Official Currency

The basic idea of a local currency is to empower people by allowing them to issue currency on the basis of the goods and services they have to offer, *i.e.* to monetize their own labor. It is hoped and expected that as the merits of local currencies and exchange become more apparent, they will, to a large extent, supplant the official currency. As this happens, one needs to consider the possible need to covert dollars to Riegels or Riegels to dollars.

It is unlikely that there will be much demand for conversion of official dollars to Riegels so long as dollars are accepted at par along with Riegels as payment for purchases within the system. The situation is similar to current foreign exchange transactions. For example, when someone from the U.S. crosses the border into Mexico to shop, they must deal with the fact that the official currency there is different from the one here, and that most items are priced in terms of "pesos." In practice, at least in the border areas, few people bother to buy pesos because the merchants almost universally accept dollars. The key issue is the exchange rate which one can get. In the case cited, the U.S. shopper can often get the same exchange rate or better (more pesos per dollar) from a merchant as s/he can get from the banks.

In the local currency case there is even less reason to convert dollars to local currency, for if the local currency is denominated in dollars, the member merchants are committed to accept it at par with the dollar, *i.e.* the exchange rate is always fixed (by the local issuing cooperative) at 1 for 1.

However, going the other way is a different matter. People prefer to **hold** dollars rather than pesos because the dollar has been debased less rapidly, *i.e.* the inflation rate in pesos has typically been much greater than the inflation rate in dollars. In other words, although the Federal Reserve has been irresponsible in its issuance of U.S. currency, the Mexican central bank has been even more irresponsible, making the holding of dollars a better inflation hedge than the holding of pesos.

If a local currency is properly issued, it should hold its value better than the dollar, but if it is denominated in dollars instead of another standard, its value will tend to change in parallel to that of the dollar. The need to exchange local currency for official currency would arise from the need for goods and services imported from outside the local system, *i.e.*, not available within the system. That is why the amount of local currency issued must be restricted, so it doesn't outrun the capacity of the local economy to produce value in the forms demanded within the local markets. The supply of Riegels needs to rise and fall **automatically** in accordance with changes in the multitude of factors which affect the local economy. Gearing the supply to the local value added, which the above formula does, assures that this will happen. The local currency needs to be insulated, as much as possible, from the adverse effects arising from manipulation of the official currency.

Two Meanings of "Dollar"

It is extremely important to distinguish between the use of the word "dollar," on the one hand to describe a unit of measure of value and, on the other, its use to describe the money issued by the Federal Reserve (the FED), either in the form of bank credit or as Federal Reserve Notes. Local exchange systems, while freeing people from using dollars, *i.e.* Federal Reserve money, typically use the dollar unit to measure the value of things traded. This makes sense because the dollar unit of measure is the unit which everyone is accustomed to using; it has meaning to people. The only problem with doing this is the fact that the dollar unit of measure is no longer defined in concrete terms. It used to be officially defined as so much fine gold, but that was abandoned long ago. The dollar is now a "rubber measuring stick" defined only by what it will buy in the market, and what it will buy in the market has been continually diminishing because of irresponsible issuance of money by the FED. That is the essence of general price inflation.

Using the dollar unit of measure, then, as a basis for valuing things creates a problem of comparability over time. A "dollar" today is not what it was yesterday, and a "dollar" tomorrow will most assuredly not be what it is today. But so long as the local currency is used only as a medium of exchange and not as a store of value, this lack of comparability over time is not much of a problem. Ideally, all currencies and exchange media should be defined in terms of some concrete standard which would establish their value along with the value of everything else being traded[108]. The existence of such a standard would make abuse and mismanagement of currencies readily apparent and allow fair exchange rates to be easily determined. It can be hoped that in the not too distant future, some organization or group will take

---

[108] Such a standard, using an assortment of basic commodities, is proposed and described in Part III of my book, *Money and Debt: A Solution to the Global Crisis.*

the initiative in defining a standard of this type. Until such time, there is little choice but to use available measures. It is possible, however, to define local standards based upon some commodity (or group of commodities) important in local commerce, such as a bushel of wheat, a kilo of rice, or a pound of copper, and there is considerable historical precedent for doing so.

Another option would be to use some other concept for valuing the things traded. Ithaca's use of the "Hour" unit is a good example. While an "Hour" is not precisely defined, people tend to think of it as having a value more or less equal to the local average hourly wage. This is what the Ithaca founders encourage, and this is what seems to be happening in practice. *Ithaca Hours* currently exchange among traders for value equivalent to about 10 dollars.

Using the hour concept instead of the dollar concept for valuing exchanges, would probably be effective in de-coupling the value of the local currency from that of the official currency. As the dollar continues to be debased, hourly wages should rise, and, one might expect, the value of the Hour currency, in terms of dollars, to rise also.

Over-accumulation -- Is It a Problem?

The question has been raised, "What if a member business has an over-accumulation of Riegels?" The answer to this lies in another question, "Why would there ever be an over-accumulation of Riegels?" A local currency, in its sole role of exchange medium, should be spent as fast as it is taken in. If a member business finds that there is not sufficient opportunity to spend Riegels on the things it needs, that would indicate that it overestimated either, (1) the value added component of its business or, (2) the willingness and/or ability of others in the community to accept Riegels. It's logical response, in either case, should be to reduce the percentage of Riegels which it is willing to accept in payment, and to use its surplus (accumulated) Riegels to reduce its commitment to the association by turning them in. This is the proper adjustment mechanism which makes the system self-regulating.

Limited or Perpetual Life?

Having a "periodic recall" feature is one way of addressing the problem of keeping the Riegels an exchange medium and limiting their use as a savings or value storage medium. As I pointed out in Part III of my book, *Money and Debt: A Solution to the Global Crisis*, I think it is very important to segregate these two functions. It is still not entirely clear how best to do this. One way to do it is to have the local currency notes expire after a certain length of time, say one year. They could all expire on the same date or the expiration dates could be staggered. Having them all expire on the same date would be too disruptive. A period of several days would have to be allowed for an orderly process of exchange to take place. Given that fact, one might just as well stretch out the time period and make it even easier by having a fraction of the issue expire each week or month throughout the year.

Comparing expiration to "demurrage," expiration can be looked at as 100% demurrage, which can, however, be avoided by spending the notes before they expire. Only members of the issuing cooperative would be unable to avoid having to exchange old notes for new. The inconvenience of having to make the exchange would probably be sufficient incentive for most (non-member) individuals to try to spend a note before expiration, even if new notes were given for old on a 1-for-1 basis. A small redemption fee might provide a further impetus for circulation.

Even as I write this, however, I'm not sure that an expiring note would work well in practice. The general public might dislike having to remain cognizant of the expiration dates of notes they hold, or taking the risk of losing out by having a note expire while in their possession. It might be best to first try a note issue which has no expiration date, or if expiration is a feature, expired notes might still hold some value, say 70% of face value, and be exchangeable for new notes at that rate.

If expiration of notes is a feature of the system, we need to consider two possibilities: (1) a member returns fewer notes than he was issued, or (2) he returns more notes than he was issued. Those members who return too few Riegels could be asked to pay the balance in dollars, or they could simply be given a smaller number of new notes to spend in the next period. However, those who return too many Riegels should **not** receive dollars for the excess. To do so would be fraught with problems, and would be counter-productive to the intention to substitute, in part, the circulation of official currency with the circulation of the local currency. They should simply be given the option of receiving new notes in an amount equivalent to the old notes surrendered and, if desired, to reduce the percentage of local currency that they agree to accept in payment for purchases in the future.

Should Interest be Charged on Balances?

In accordance with the principles outlined earlier, there should be no interest charged on lines of credit or notes issued to members. Since no one has made any sacrifice, there is no entitlement to interest. The costs of operating the system should be borne by all members in proportion to the benefits they derive from using the system. With this in mind, it makes sense to levy membership fees in proportion to the amount of notes issued to each member. This may look like interest but it is not. The association, after all, is not a profit-making entity and it need only collect enough to cover the costs of operating the system.

There's no reason, of course, why a ledger system can not operate in conjunction with a local currency. That's precisely what the LETSonora system does. LETSonora started as a typical LETS system with a computerized ledger system and a telephone answering system for reporting transactions to the registrar. In an attempt to make the reporting of transactions more efficient, transaction record forms similar to bank checks were later developed. These transaction record forms would be filled out like a check and given to the seller who would then deliver them to the registrar to have the credit recorded. Finally, to further reduce the bookkeeping burden, circulating notes were issued. Figures 16.1 and 16.2 show the front and reverse sides, respectively, of a LETS Receipt used by LETSonora.

The mechanics of these options are essentially the same as present banking practice, in which a member can either "deposit" credits (get a credit to his/her LETS account) or take them in the form of paper notes.

Figure 16.2: A LETSonora Receipt -- Face Side

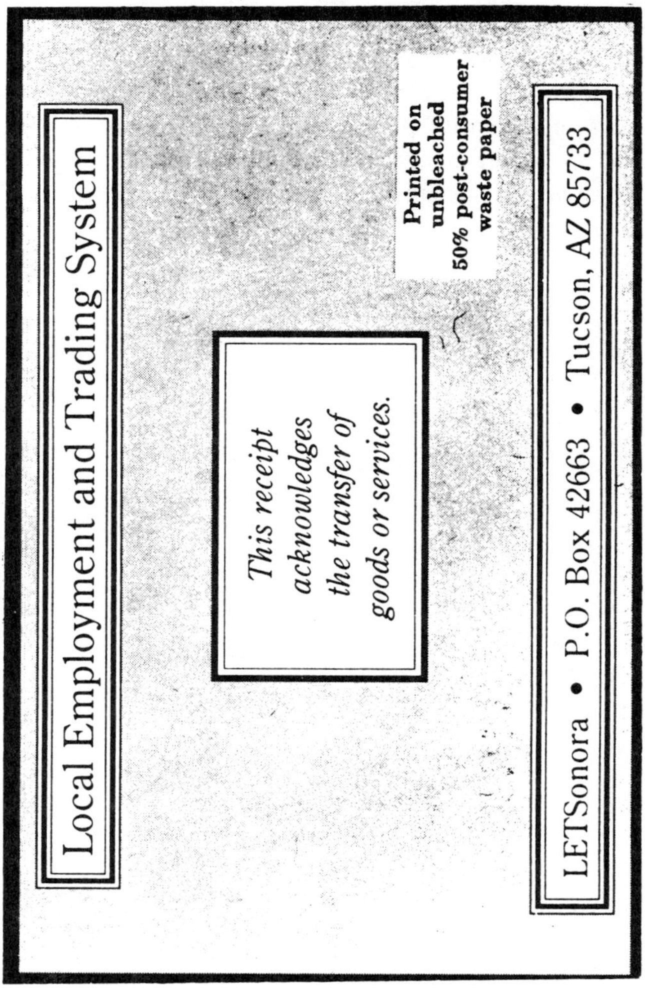

Figure 16.1: A LETSonora Receipt -- Reverse Side

Similar approaches are also being taken elsewhere.

As the dominant institutions of industrial civilization continue to decay, and as more people find themselves pushed to the margins of the money economy, pressure will build for the implementation of alternatives. True democracy can only be forged within the economic realm, and money and exchange are the key elements which must be democratized. Local currency and exchange systems that are equitable and just will be essential in assuring that the transition will be smooth and peaceful.

APPENDIX A: NOTE ON BANKING AS A PROFESSION AND ITS REFORM

This note is based on material contained in an article, "The Nature of Banking" by Dr. Ralph Borsodi, which appeared in *Green Revolution*, Vol. 34, No. 10, December 1977, published by the School of Living, RD1, Box 185A, Cochranville, PA 19330.

Borsodi outlines the following principles which he sees as necessary in reforming the banking profession.

> "1. Banking is a profession and not a business. The Banker, like the lawyer and the doctor, unless he stultifies himself, must put the trust reposed in him before anything else. We entrust our health and even our lives to our doctor. We entrust vital rights and our material interests to our lawyer. We entrust our money and our savings to our banker. The banker is a trustee, and he has not more moral right to exploit the funds entrusted to him than a doctor has the right to exploit the sickness of his patients, or a lawyer the difficulties of his clients. *Professional compensation is one thing, but maximizing profits is something altogether different* [emphasis added].
>
> 2. Bankers, like lawyers and doctors, should therefore be licensed and only those qualified to study (usually at an accredited university) and who observe professional standards both in their practice and in their charges for their services, should be permitted by law to engage in banking.[109]

---

[109] I disagree with Borsodi's reliance upon licensing statutes and their enforcement by the state as a means of maintaining professional standards. Licensing often leads to restraint of trade and extortionate fees. It can also be argued that most licenses are a violation of basic human rights guaranteed by the constitution. I favor the elimination of such statutory privileges and prefer to rely upon (1) open access to information, (2) consumer education, and (3) the certification of practitioners by private accrediting agencies. As Borsodi himself proposes below, banks should not be operated as corporate businesses. Without the limited liability protection afforded by the corporate umbrella, banks would tend to be smaller, local in scope, and more responsive to the needs of their clients. If the establishment of banks (or the exchange systems which might succeed them) was less restricted and the depository function was handled by other agencies, the potential for currency abuse would be greatly constrained.

> 3. The banker, by the essential nature of the service he renders, is a fiduciary trustee. It is malpractice for him to do anything with the funds entrusted to him which he ought to know should not be done with them, just as it is malpractice for a doctor to prescribe treatments which he ought to know endanger the health of his patients. Nobody, no matter how great the profit, has a moral right to betray those who trust him. It is betrayal to exploit the opportunity for profit which trust in his integrity creates.
>
> 4. Bankers should not be granted charters to operate banks as business corporations; they should not be legally authorized to earn profits for stockholders because corporations limit the liabilities of those who own them. In practice the law makes it virtually impossible to hold corporate officers and directors liable for what I am calling malpractice.
>
> Banks should be owned and operated by sole proprietors, by partnerships, by mutual and cooperative associations; and all those who own them and conduct them should be personally responsible and accountable for the safety of the funds entrusted to them. All laws which exempt bankers, as would be true of all laws which exempted any kind of professional person from full liability for his or her practices, are morally null and void."

Borsodi also enumerates a number of measures which he thinks would eliminate inflation, reduce unemployment, end the boom and bust business cycle, reduce speculation, provide for the capital needs of the local community, and prevent the government "from using the banks of the nation to indulge in its present extravagances by forcing them to finance its deficits."

He argues that, if the following measures were taken, *the whole moral climate of the economy would be transformed*:

> "1. Bankers, as professionals, should ensure both the safety and proper use of the funds entrusted to them.

2. Professional bankers should see to it that the funds entrusted to them be used only to facilitate commerce.

3. Professional bankers should give priority to financing local needs before investing in projects outside the community.

4. Professional bankers should take over the whole field of investment, taking it 'out of the hands of the so-called investment bankers of Wall Street.'"

It is encouraging to note some movement in this direction by a few "enlightened" bankers. There are some notable examples of banks which, while still operating under the umbrella of the corporate charter, have acted to implement some of the above proposals, especially the financing of local needs. Among these are the South Shore Bank in Chicago and the Community Capital Bank of Brooklyn. Besides these, there are dozens of non-bank community loan funds springing up all over the country. For more information about these, contact the National Association of Community Development Loan Funds, P.O. Box 40085, Philadelphia, PA 19106.

APPENDIX B: NOTE ON THE PROPER BASIS OF ISSUE FOR CURRENCY AND THE MEANS OF FINANCING CAPITAL INVESTMENTS AND CONSUMER DURABLES[110]

At any given time, there is flow of goods and services coming to market. The problem which the instrument called money seeks to solve is to provide each person who has a part in its production with a means of acquiring his/her share of the total value. Col. Harwood describes the typical money creation process which prevailed prior to World War I. While banking had serious problems even then, sound principles on the basis of issue were still being followed by most of the larger banks.

> "As a manufacturer shipped completed things to market, he would prepare a document describing the shipment, take it to his bank, and borrow purchasing media that, in practical effect represented the things en route to market. The bank made the loan by crediting an appropriate amount to the checking account of the manufacturer, but this amount was not deducted from other checking account liabilities of the bank. Thus new purchasing media were created and were placed in circulation when the manufacturer used the addition to his checking account to pay wages, salaries, suppliers, and other costs of processing the things sent to market. (As the things were sold, the receipts from sales were used to repay the bank loan by having that amount deducted from the manufacturer's account. Thus the purchasing media created for temporary use were withdrawn when their purpose had been served.)
>
> "Those who received the newly issued purchasing media from the manufacturer then could choose whatever they wanted that the markets offered... The procedure described above has been modified in recent decades as mass production has developed on a broader scale and now occurs almost continuously throughout the year. ...

---

[110] This section is based on material contained in an article, "The Lost Art of Commercial Banking" by E. C. Harwood, in *How Safe Is Your Bank*, published by the American Institute for Economic Research, Great Barrington, MA 01230, 1989. All quoted passages in the following text are taken from that article which was originally published in 1974.

"The automobile manufacturer arranges with a commercial bank for a 'line of credit' and gives a promissory note that may be paid off only once each year during the model changeover period when no cars are en rout to markets. Thus a series of loans continually being repaid as cars are sold is replaced by a single borrowing resulting in the creation of purchasing media that remain in circulation as long as the flow of cars to markets continues...

"As commercial banking developed, especially in the United States, two quite different functions have been performed by the same institutions. In addition to the commercial banking function already described, most banks performed an investment function, accepting saved purchasing media and investing it.

"The borrower from the bank in the savings-investment transaction is *not* at that time sending to or otherwise offering things of equal value in the markets to be sold. He does not desire purchasing media so that he may distribute it to employees and suppliers who participated in preparing things *for* the markets. His desire is to claim things *from* the markets, either equipment for his factory or a new car for personal use, or any of the multitude of other things available, such as new bricks for construction of a factory, etc. Consequently, the bank should not create new purchasing media for such a borrower but should lend him purchasing media already in existence that some present owner or owners save and deposit in the bank.

"Probably because the same banks have been performing two functions, each of which involves lender-borrower transactions, similar forms (such as promissory notes), and related procedures, many bankers have confused the two functions. .. In the first type of procedure, the new purchasing media created represented the exchange value of things en route to or being offered for sale in the local markets; however, in the second, the new purchasing media represented things (such as land, factories, or consumer goods) not being offered by the borrowers for sale but on the contrary being removed by them from the markets.

"Perhaps the clearest example of the confusion between commercial and non-commercial banking is provided by the financing of automobiles in or en route to markets in contrast with consumer installment borrowing to purchase a new car. The important distinction that makes all the difference between sound and unsound commercial banking is:

a. When an automobile manufacturer borrows newly created purchasing media and distributes them to employees, suppliers, and others, he is arranging for those potential buyers to obtain their shares (in dollar value) of things in or en route to markets.

b. When an installment buyer arranges to purchase a car [with money he/she borrows], he is not claiming a share corresponding to his participation in producing things for markets, he is claiming someone else's share." [In order for this to be possible, someone else must be willing to forego claiming his share for the term of the loan, *i.e.* be desirous of saving his share rather than spending it. -- t.g.]

"Thus, one can see that a bank's lending transaction may reflect additional things offered in the markets *or it may not*. If it does, creation of new purchasing media (for use until retired by repayment of the loan by the seller) is sound commercial banking. If the lending transaction does *not reflect additional* offerings in the markets, it should be financed by the savings-investment procedures."

The above makes clear that there are two very different things going on in commercial banking. Commercial banks have the primary responsibility of issuing new money into circulation, which they do by making loans. They also act as depositories, accepting deposits of existing money which people and businesses wish to save. This money is held as "reserves" against which new loans are made. Much of the problem seems to stem from confusion caused by the fact that the terminology, forms and procedures for the two functions are the same. It would probably be best to completely divorce the creation of new exchange media from any association with the borrowing-lending process.

SOURCES AND RESOURCES

Contacts -- U.S. and Canada

COMMUNITY INFORMATION RESOURCE CENTER
P.O. Box 42663
Tucson, AZ 85733
CIRC can also be reached on-line via MCI mail:CIRC.

Operating as a project of NEST, Inc., an Arizona non-profit, tax-exempt corporation, CIRC seeks to promote community health and positive change by supporting the emergence of mutual support structures, participatory democracy, local self-reliance, appropriate technology, sustainable living, and micro-enterprise.

CIRC is a networking hub, an information source, and a support organization. It provides organizing assistance, administrative support, instruction, access to computer and telecommunications technologies, opinion and market surveys, interdisciplinary research, and data analysis. Besides it regional activities, CIRC networks nationally and globally with groups concerned with intentional community, community economics, appropriate technology, right-livelihood, and sustainable living.

School of Living
RD 1, Box 185A
Cochranville, PA 19330

Since 1934, the School of Living has been promoting right-livelihood, decentralism, social justice, sustainable economics, communities, and cooperative self-reliance. It publishes a quarterly journal, the *Green Revolution*.

E.F. Schumacher Society
RD 3, Box 76
Great Barrington, MA 01230

Founded in memory of the author of *Small is Beautiful*, the Schumacher Society, like the School of Living, works to foster appropriate technology, human scale, and right-livelihood.

Ithaca MONEY
Box 6578
Ithaca, NY 14851

Ithaca MONEY is a tabloid newspaper which issues *Ithaca HOUR* notes to its advertisers. It provides information about local exchange and self-help options. Communities wishing to institute similar programs can obtain a "Home Town Money Starter Kit" for $25 or 2 1/2 *Ithaca HOURS*. The kit includes "all start-up and maintenance procedures, forms, laws, news articles, computer programs, updates and an *Ithaca MONEY* subscription.

Boulder Barter Network
P.O. Box 441
Boulder, CO 80306

Operates in a manner similar to *Ithaca MONEY.* Publishes a tabloid newspaper called the *Boulder Barter Directory*, and issues circulating *Boulder HOUR* notes.

Time Dollar Network
P.O. Box 42160
Washington, DC 20015 Tel.: (202) 686-5200

National clearinghouse for information about service credit/time dollar programs, including a directory and organizing assistance.

National Association of Community Development Loan Funds
P.O. Box 40085
Philadelphia, PA 19106

Provides information about and directory of Community Development Loan Funds.

EcoNet/PeaceNet
Institute for Global Communications
18 De Boom Street
San Francisco, CA 94107 Tel.: (415) 442-0220

Provides facilities for telecommunications networking. If you have a personal computer and a modem, you have the world at your fingertips. EcoNet and PeaceNet provide access via electronic mail to subscribers of various networks around the world. It also maintains public conferences on hundreds of topics, which provide valuable information and discussion opportunities. EcoNet includes two conferences which provide on-going dialogue opportunities relating to LETS system developments. Can.lets and oz.lets focus on developments in Canada and Australia, respectively.

In Canada, these same conferences can be accessed through the WEB.
Contact:
WEB
401 Richmond St. W., Suite 104
Toronto, ON M5V 3A8, Canada Tel.: (416) 596-0212

LANDSMAN COMMUNITY SERVICES, LTD.
1660 Embelton Cres.
Courtenay, BC V9N 6N8, Canada Tel.: (604) 338-0213/0214

LANDSMAN is operated by Michael Linton, originator of LETS. This is the definitive source for information about LETS theory and operation. Michael is available to work with groups who wish to set-up a LETS system. He has developed a simulation game called "LETSPlay," as well as software needed for computerized operation of a LETsystem. New improved accounting software, called "NLETS," has recently been developed by Michael Linton and Richard Knights.

Greg Meadows
K-W LETSystem
Box 26008
Kitchener, ON N2G 4V8 Canada

Greg Meadows who runs the Kitchener-Waterloo LETSystem is perhaps the most active current LETS networker in North America. He is a valuable source of information for anyone wishing to start a LETS system. He has developed a simulation game and edits the K-W LETSystem newsletter. K-W offers "Founding Framework" documents and information package. User's and Administration manuals are available on 5 1/4 inch diskette for $20 (Canadian). K-W LETS also has a bibliography of magazine and newspaper clippings, popular and academic essays on LETS, and overseas LETS information.

Tim Inkpen
545 Sherbourne St., Apt. 1107
Toronto, ON M4X 1W5 Canada

Tim Inkpen is the communications coordinator and outreach person for LETS in Toronto. He is a valuable source of LETS information.

David Badke
Box 89
Silverton, BC V0G 2B0 Canada

Provides accounting software called LETSBase.

American Institute for Economic Research
Great Barrington, MA 01230

Provides an un-orthodox perspective on topics such as money and the economy.

International Reciprocal Trade Association
9513 Beach Mill Road
Great Falls, VA 22066 Tel.:(703) 759-1473

Trade association for the commercial barter industry.

Missouri Community Economic Development
628 Clark Hall, University of Missouri
Columbia, MO 65211.

Provides information and assistance on community economic development strategies.

Oregon Marketplace
1004 W. 23rd Ave., Suite 300
Portland, OR 97210.

Assists communities with "buy local" programs and import substitution.

Industrial Cooperative Association (ICA)
Community Economic Development Program
58 Day St., Suite 203
Somerville, MA 02144.

Provides information and assistance in forming cooperatives and community economic development.

Some Known LETS systems in the United States and Canada

Eugene LETS Network
Eugene, OR
(no address available)
(503) 688-6595

Eaglestar LETSystem
19655 Campbell Road
Black Forest, CO 80909

L.A. LETSystem
c/o CRSP
3551 White House Place
Los Angeles, CA 90004

LETS in Toronto
44 St. George St. #303
Toronto, ON M5S 2E4 Canada

Guelph LETS
9 Macdonnell St.
Guelph, ON N1H 2Z2 Canada

Sudbury Employment and Trading System (SETS)
176 Larch St., Suite 302
Sudbury, ON P3E 1C6 Canada

Sangeen Trading Community
RR 3
Chesley, ON N0G 1L0 Canada

Victoria LETS
Box 5525, Stn. B
Victoria, BC V8R 6S4 Canada

Duncan LETS
c/o 5364 River Bottom Road, RR #2
Duncan, BC V9L 1N9 Canada

Women's LETSystem
1660 Embelton Cres.
Courtenay, BC V9N 6N8 Canada

K-W LETSystem
Box 1731
Kitchener, ON N2G 4R3 Canada

Contacts -- Australia and New Zealand

John Zube
Libertarian Microfiche Publishing Company
7 Oxley St.
Berrima, NSW 2577 Australia

This is a unique and phenomenal source of material on free money, free banking, alternative exchange, and decentralism. Zube has converted to microfiche form more than 300,000 pages of material, much of which is primary resource material (letters, unpublished papers) which are hard to find or not available elsewhere.

New Zealand GREEN$QUARTERLY
P.O. Box 21140
Christchurch, New Zealand Tel.: (03) 661-992

GREEN$QUARTERLY provides a comprehensive assemblage of information collected from the various LETS systems operating in New Zealand (41 at last count). This source is a "must" for anyone wishing to keep up on LETS system developments and "mutual credit," in general. G$Q provides information about how actual operating systems have dealt with various problems and concerns. It also provides access to resource materials such as new software and a "Management Guide."

OZLETS
P.O. Box 1640
Armidale, NSW 2350
Australia

National publication for LETS organizers in Australia and overseas.

Blue Mountains LETS
P.O. Box 125
Katoomba 2780
Australia Tel.:(047)82 3309, 82 6685.

Blue Mountains is one of the largest LETS systems in the world with over 1500 members.

Kevin O'Brien
157 Jackson St.
Petone, New Zealand

Offers LETS software called "Gnomes of Zurich."

John Lowe
Wai-iti Farms
RD 1
Hastings, New Zealand

Has developed updated LETS accounting software using D-BASE III.

John Croft
Dept. of State Development
P.O. Box 7234
Cloister's Square, Perth, Western Australia 6850
Australia

Offers LETS Training Manual for AUS$20.

Teranaki Green Dollars
P.O. Box 274
New Plymouth, New Zealand

Offers Green Dollar Management Guide for NZ$25.

Contacts -- United Kingdom

LETSLink UK Network
61 Woodcock Road
Warminster, Wiltshire BA12 9DH
Great Britain

A "network for the LETSystem, which keeps groups and individuals in touch with LETS developments around the country." Offers a variety of resources and documentation, including a newsletter, a LETS "STARTER PACK" (for £5), and a UK contact list (for 4 first class stamps).

Richard Knights
31D High Street
Totnes, Devon TQ9 5PH
Great Britain

Offers a new version of LETS accounting software and user's manual for £30 and £10, respectively.

Steve Watson
Brighton, Sussex
England
(no other address available)
Tel.: 011 44(273) 689 567

Offers Apple Mac LETS accounting software.

REFERENCES

"A Public Service Economy: An Interview with Edgar S. Cahn." *Multinational Monitor*, April 1989, pp. 17-21.

Berry, Wendell, "Does Community Have a Value?," in *Home Economics: Fourteen Essays*. New York: Farrar, Straus and Giroux, 1987.

Bilgram, Hugo, and L. E. Levy, *The Cause of Business Depressions*. Philadelphia: J. B. Lippincott Company, 1914. Also, reprinted by Libertarian Book House, Bombay, India, 1950.

Borsodi, Ralph, *Inflation and the Coming Keynesian Catastrophe*: *The Story of the Exeter Experiment With Constants*. Published jointly by The E. F. Schumacher Society, RD 3, Box 76, Great Barrington, MA 01230 and the School of Living, RD 1, Box 185A, Cochranville, PA 19330, 1989.

---- *This Ugly Civilization*. New York: Simon and Schuster, 1929. (Also Harper, 1933).

---- *Flight From The City*. New York: Harper, 1933

Cahn, Edgar S., "Time Dollars." *Co-op America Quarterly*, Spring 1993.

Cole, G.D.H., and W. Mellor, *The Meaning of Industrial Freedom*. London: Geo. Allen and Unwin, Ltd., 1918.

Del Mar, Alexander, *The History of Money in America: From the Earliest Times to the Establishment of the Constitution*. Hawthorne, CA: Omni Publications, 1966. Originally published 1899.

Directory of Volunteer Service Credit Programs. College Park, MD: University of Maryland, Center on Aging, April 1993.

Dunkman, William, *Money, Credit and Banking*. New York: Random House, 1970.

Fisher, Irving, *Stamp Scrip*. New York: Adelphi Company, 1933.

Fromm, Erich, *The Sane Society*. Greenwich, CT: Fawcett Publications, Inc., 1955.

Gesell, Silvio, *The Natural Economic Order*. San Antonio, TX: The Free Economy Publishing Co., 1934. (Translated from the sixth German edition). Originally published in 1913.

Greco, Thomas H., Jr., *Money and Debt: A Solution to the Global Crisis*. Second edition, Thomas H. Greco, Publisher, P.O. Box 42663, Tucson, AZ 85733, 1990.

Gregg, Richard, *The Big Idol*. Navajivan Press, Ahmedabad-14, India, 1963.

Harwood, E. C., "The Lost Art of Commercial Banking," in *How Safe Is Your Bank*. Great Barrington, MA: American Institute for Economic Research, 1989.

Hayek, Friedrich von, *Choice in Currency: A Way to Stop Inflation*. London: Institute of Economic Affairs, 1976.

Hobson, Ruth, "The Amazing Growth of LETS in the UK." *LETSlink Newsletter* (UK), May, 1993.

Kennedy, Margrit, *Interest and Inflation Free Money*. Permakultur Institut e.V., Ginsterweg 5, D-3074 Steyerberg, West Germany, 1988.

Kohr, Leopold, *The Breakdown of Nations*. New York: E.P. Dutton, 1957, 1978.

Linton, Michael, and Thomas Greco, "The Local Employment and Trading System." *Whole Earth Review*, No. 55, Summer 1987.

Lovelock, James, *The Ages of Gaia*. New York: Norton, 1988.

---- *Healing Gaia: A New Prescription for the Living Planet*. New York: Crown Publishing Group, 1991.

Max-Neef, Manfred, "Reflections on a Paradigm Shift in Economics," in *The New Economic Agenda*. Mary Inglis and Sandra Kramer (Eds.), Findhorn Press, The Park, Forres IV36 OTZ, Scotland, 1985.

Mitchell, Ralph A. and Neil Shafer, *Standard Catalog of Depression Scrip of the United States: The 1930s Including Canada and Mexico*. First edition, Iola, Wisconsin: Kraus Publications, 1984.

Modern Money Mechanics. Federal Reserve Bank of Chicago, 1992.

Naisbitt, John, *Megatrends*. New York: Warner Books, 1982.

Narayan, R.K., *The Financial Expert*. Chicago: University of Chicago Press, 1981.

Reinfeld, Fred, *The Story of Paper Money*. New York: Sterling Publishing Co., Inc., 1957.

Reissig, Jose', "Bonds That Brought a Boom." *New Economics*, #20, Winter 1991 (London, England).

Riegel, E. C., *Flight From Inflation: The Monetary Alternative*. The Heather Foundation, Box 4, Waterford, VA 22190, 1978.

---- *Private Enterprise Money: A Non-Political Money System*. New York: Harbinger House, 1944.

Rueff, Jacques, *The Age of Inflation*. Tr. A. H. Meeus and F. G. Clarke, Chicago: Henry Regnery Co., 1964.

---- *The Monetary Sin of the West*. New York: Macmillan, 1972.

Sale, Kirkpatrick, *Human Scale*. New York: Coward, McCann & Geoghegan, 1980.

Soddy, Frederick, *Wealth, Virtual Wealth and Debt*. Third edition, Hawthorne, CA: Omni Publications, 1961. Reprinted from the second edition, 1933.

Soddy, Frederick, *The Role of Money*. New York: Harcourt, 1935.

Suplizio, Paul E., *Commercial Barter Exchanges in Society*, an address presented to the Chicago Association of Commerce and Industry, Chicago, September 18, 1985. International Reciprocal Trade Association, 9513 Beach Mill Road, Great Falls, VA 22066, 1985.

The Federal Reserve System: Purposes and Functions. Board of Governors of the Federal Reserve System, Washington, DC 1961.

Thoren, Margaret, *Figuring Out The FED*. Truth in Money, Inc., P.O. Box 30, Chagrin Falls, OH 44022, 1985, 1993.

Thoren, Theodore, and Richard Warner, *The Truth In Money Book*. Revised second edition, Truth in Money, Inc., P.O. Box 30, Chagrin Falls, OH 44022, 1984.

Two Faces of Debt. Federal Reserve Bank of Chicago, 1992.

The Commercial Barter Industry. IRTA Fact Sheet, International Reciprocal Trade Association, 9513 Beach Mill Road, Great Falls, VA 22066.

The International Reciprocal Trade Association. IRTA Fact Sheet, International Reciprocal Trade Association, 9513 Beach Mill Road, Great Falls, VA 22066.

INDEX